The Mission of Human and Christian Education

The Gospel Journey of John Baptist de La Salle

Jacques Goussin fsc

English Translation edited by
Gerard Rummery fsc

Translated by
Finian Allman fsc
Christian Moe fsc
Julian Watson fsc

Lasallian Education Services
Melbourne Australia

First published in 2003 by
Lasallian Education Services
PO Box 77   East Bentleigh
Victoria 3165   Australia
Tel +61 3 9570 8866 Fax +61 3 9570 8008

Cover illustration: Stained glass window from Oakhill Chapel, Castle Hill, Sydney
Design and production by David Lovell Publishing
Typeset in 11/14 Garamond
Printed & bound in Australia by Openbook Print 1315-03

National Library of Australia
Cataloguing-in-Publication data

Goussin, Jacques FSC.
   [Construire l'homme at dire Dieu à lécole English]
   The Mission of human and Christian education : the gospel
   journey of John Baptist de La Salle.

   ISBN 0 9751148 0 8.

   1. La Salle, Jean Baptiste de, Saint, 1651–1719. 2.
   Christian education – Early works to 1800. 3. Christian
   saints – France – Biography. I. Title.

271.78

Author's Foreword

The life journey of John Baptist de La Salle gives us cause for wonder and admiration, for far from exploiting the gifts with which nature had endowed him for his own advantage, he lived a life which ran counter to that of his contemporaries.

In a society where the prevailing ambition was to reach a higher status or to amass greater wealth, he displayed a degree of humility that bordered on destitution and abjection. In a society which passed from a charitable welcome to the poor to rejecting them and confining them in the General Hospital, De La Salle pushed his solicitude for them even to the point of sharing their poverty and ranking himself among their number. When, for example, he wrote to Brother Gabriel Drolin on 4 September 1705 'I have to adjust my accounts day by day', he had been reduced to the situation of an artisan or day labourer.[1]

In a society which gave the people the help of religion but denied them the advantage of knowledge, De La Salle asserted 'how important it is for an artisan to know how to read and write, since granted the little ability he may have, by knowing how to read and write well, he is capable of anything.'[2] Without separating himself from the prejudices of his time which demanded that status in society should show and effect the order willed by God (whereby each person should remain in the condition destined by his birth), De La Salle brought about a real cultural shift 'by the establishment of the Christian schools, where the teaching is offered free of charge and entirely for the glory of God, where the children are kept all day, learn to read, to write and to know their religion, and are always kept busy, so that when their parents want them to go to work they are prepared for employment.'[3]

De La Salle's is certainly a most human journey but it would be more exact to call it a spiritual journey. The word 'conversion' traditionally used to describe such a life expresses De La Salle's Spirit-filled life with complete accuracy. He himself explained it in the following terms:

'God [who] wishes all to be saved,[4] who guides all things with wisdom and serenity, whose way it is not to force the inclinations of anyone, willed to commit me entirely to the development of the schools.'[5]

In following out his dialogue with the Divine Will, De La Salle practised the two virtues that he bequeathed to his Brothers: an ardent faith whereby he sought the Will of God in the unfolding of events, and an unwearying zeal by means of which after discerning that same will he sought to carry it into effect by the best kind of Gospel response. In this way he moved from a 'church of the establishment' to a 'church founded on Providence alone'; from a 'church as institution' to a 'church as missionary;' from a 'governing church' to a 'servant church.'

How then did it happen that this man, raised in accordance with the religious principles of middle-class Rheims, introduced into the elite group of the clergy of France in the seminary of Saint Sulpice, concerned to fulfil all the duties of a Canon of Rheims Cathedral conscientiously and with dignity, someone whom we might rightly have expected to be called to figure among the great bishops of the time, happens not only to have established an association of lay people dedicated to Christian education but above all to have bound himself to that association and to have lived and to have died as one of its members?

Clarifying the *how* of the above question should enable us at the same time to clarify the *why*, that is to say, to turn a light upon the wellsprings of the Saint's inspiration, upon the master plan that guided and sustained his enthusiasm, his reasons for the choices he made and the direction he willed to give to his life's work: in a word, to give an overall interpretation of his life.

Jacques Goussin

Contents

Introduction

It was my privilege to have met Brother Jacques Goussin when he attended the International Lasallian Studies Session (SIEL) in Rome in 1989–1990. I came to appreciate the way in which he brought his background in anthropology to his study of the man, John Baptist de La Salle, and to his understanding of the work of this saintly man and his first followers.

I am now pleased to be able to offer English-speaking readers a translation of Brother Jacques' book *Construire l'homme et dire Dieu à l'École: Jean-Baptiste de La Salle*, which could be translated fairly literally as *Building up the human and speaking of God in the school*, although the translation misses the subtlety of the original. In order to do justice to the two ideas of the original French, I am using as the English title an important phrase taken from the 1987 Rule of the De La Salle Brothers, namely, that 'the purpose of this Institute is to give *a human and Christian education* [my emphasis] to the young, especially the poor, according to the ministry which the Church has entrusted to it'. A major insight of Lasallian scholarship over the past 50 years has been the recognition of De La Salle's holistic contribution to education by his insistence in offering (contrary to the usage of his time) a practical education through the vernacular to *the children of the artisans and the poor*. In practice, this meant responding to the real needs of poor children in very diverse situations, not only by making them literate but also in such particular ways as teaching elementary navigation to the children of fishermen in Calais and Boulogne, and training the children of merchants and workers in Paris and Rouen in elementary accounting.

Each of the ten chapters of the book tells the story of how John Baptist de La Salle developed a clear vision of what he felt was needed for the education of poor boys in his native France. His founding of what was to become after his death an international brotherhood devoted to a particular way of teaching poor boys was a long struggle against entrenched interests in the Church and the society of his time. The continuing existence of this movement in over eighty countries in today's world shows the enduring value of this educational vision.

The book is valuable because it appeals at many different levels. It is primarily a human story, that of a great man who left his own privileged position in society to offer a practical education especially directed to the sons of workers and the urban poor. At another level, it is the story of a saintly man who saw the value of his life in following what he was to call the 'guidance' [*conduite*] of God through events and circumstances. At a third level, it offers scope for profound reflection on *why* De La Salle acted as he did, because the author has assembled at the end of each chapter various texts from De La Salle's own writings over his long life, so that we are able to appreciate the consistency of his thinking and the profound reasons which led him to act as he did. Assembling these texts around certain moments in De La Salle's life, as the author has done, makes them more readily accessible to readers in English who do not have easy access to more recent translations into English. At the end of Chapter 10 there is a detailed series of themes and syntheses which in this edition have been assembled under the general title of an Appendix.

My thanks go in a very special way to the author, Frère Jacques Goussin, for his permission to translate his work into English. As the Lasallian province or District of Australia, New Zealand and Papua New Guinea nears its centenary in 2006, I am very conscious of the historical debt we owe to those seven French Brothers who were part of the original foundation in Australia even if circumstances prevented them from staying. It is both an acknowledgement of our French origins as a congregation and an appreciation for the heritage which our French Brothers such as the author, Jacques Goussin, continue to share with us that Brothers Julian Watson, Christian Moe and Finian Allman willingly shared the task of translation from the original French. Their appreciation of the value of the text, and the enthusiasm and encouragement they brought to the task, made my own work as overall editor much easier.

The District of Australia, New Zealand and Papua-New Guinea has its own Lasallian iconography, some examples of which have been used to illustrate sections of this book. We are especially indebted to Carolyne Vumbaca of Oakhill College for her photographs of some of the scenes from De La Salle's life as depicted in the stained glass of the Oakhill Chapel, to Leopoldine Mimovich for the reproduction of her bas relief commemorating the 90 years of De La Salle College Malvern, to Michael Galovic for his icon of De La Salle, and to De La Salle Malvern for permission to reproduce the symbolic painting presented to the College by former student Eric Nilan to honour the tercentenary of the birth of John Baptist de La Salle in 1951.

I would like to acknowledge the courtesy of Brother Jacques d'Huiteau, Visitor of the French District, which holds the copyright for the original text, in granting his approval for this translation.

Brother Gerard Rummery

Notes on Sources

As the work which follows is a translation from the French, references are as far as possible to works which have English translations. In the case of references to some *Cahiers lasalliens*, however, the reference is given to the original French document if there is no official English translation. *Cahiers lasalliens* is a continuing series of studies in French, which so far has published in critical editions

— the earliest *princeps* editions of De La Salle's published works;

— studies of important individual writings, e.g., a comparison of the 1706 manuscript edition of *The Conduct of Schools* with the first printed edition of 1720;

— detailed studies of De La Salle's administration of his father's estate when he was named executor of his will before attaining his majority;

— studies of the sources of some of De La Salle's writings.

Biographies

Blain, Jean Baptiste, *The Life of John Baptist de La Salle, Founder of the Institute of the Brothers of the Christian Schools*. A biography in three books. Translated by Richard Arnandez FSC. Edited by Luke Salm FSC. Lasallian Publications, Landover, Maryland, 2000.

Blain, Jean Baptiste, *The Mind and Heart of St John Baptist de La Salle, 1651–1719, according to his Earliest Published Biographer*. A Translation with Introduction and Notes by Edwin Bannon FSC, Lasallia, De La Salle Publications, Oxford.

Maillefer, Dom Elie, *The Life of John Baptist de La Salle*. Translated by William Quinn FSC. Revised translation with notes by Donald C. Mouton FSC. Lasallian Publications, Landover, Maryland, 1996.

Bernard, Brother, *The Admirable Guidance shown by Divine Providence in the person of the Venerable Servant of God, John Baptist de La Salle, Founder of the Institute of the Brothers of the Christian Schools.* Manuscript of 1721. Translated by Donald C. Mouton FSC. Lasallian Publications, Landover, Maryland, 1996.

Fitzpatrick, Edward A., *La Salle, Patron of All Teachers.* The Bruce Publishing Company, Milwaukee, 1951.

Memoir on the Habit, pp.190-195.

Published works of John Baptist de La Salle (in English) from which citations are made

Collection of Various Short Treatises. Translated by W.J. Battersby FSC. Edited by Daniel Bourke FSC. Lasallian Publications, Landover, Maryland, 1993.

The Conduct of the Christian Schools. Translated by F. De La Fontanerie and Richard Arnandez FSC. Edited by William Mann FSC. Lasallian Publications, Landover, Maryland, 1996.

Meditations. Translated by Richard Arnandez FSC and Augustine Loes FSC. Edited by Francis Heuther FSC and Augustine Loes FSC. Christian Brothers Conference, Landover, Maryland, 1994.

Note: Citations from the Meditations *give the number of the meditation followed by the number of the point [1, 2 or 3] referred to.* Meditations for the Time of Retreat *nos. 193-208, are indicated as MTR.*

The Letters of John Baptist de La Salle. Translation, Introduction and Commentary by Colman Molloy FSC. Edited with additional Commentary by Augustine Loes FSC. Lasallian Publications, Romeoville, Illinois, 1988.

Letters and Documents *(Memoir on the Habit—Mémoire sur l'Habit).* Translated and edited by W.J. Battersby FSC. Longmans, Green & Co, London, 1952.

Abbreviations

Throughout the text, and particularly in the Notes, the following abbreviations are used:

MTR — Meditations in the Time of Retreat

CL — Cahiers lasalliens

Chapter 1

Paths leading
to school

1. A priestly vocation welcomed

The biographers of John Baptist de La Salle agree in recognizing in him both wisdom and piety, the one as precocious as the other. According to Maillefer, 'from his early days he enjoyed the serious occupations of prayer and the reading of good books'.[1] Blain goes further: 'In him nothing childish could be observed ... and piety, which in most of us is a late-maturing fruit of grace, appeared in him before the use of reason'.[2]

So we must not be surprised if very early on he 'felt himself attracted to consecrate himself to God in the priesthood. He counted on the religious spirit of his parents to put no obstacle in his way although he was the oldest of his brothers. In fact they agreed to his suggestion of receiving the tonsure. This appeared to him as a worthy motive for loving the Church'.[3]

Responding to the call of God, young John Baptist took his decision and told his parents. Without doubt the firmness of his determination led to their acquiescence. But at the same time the certainty that they would give their consent and the absolute confidence he had in the depth of their faith could only reinforce his plan. In his heart his assurance became their wish.

The project became a reality on 11 March 1662, seven weeks before his eleventh birthday. On the very next day he went back to his studies at the *Collège des Bons Enfants*, sporting with simplicity the tonsure, the sign of the service he had decided on.

De La Salle receives a canonry

Four years later, on 9 July 1666, the first cousin of John Baptist's grandfather, Pierre Dozet, Archdeacon of Champagne and Chancellor of Rheims University, resigned his position of canon in John Baptist's favour and he took possession of it on 7 January 1667. He turned sixteen four months later.

To record this event the three biographers of the saint, Bernard, Maillefer and Blain make use of the same expression, 'he received a canonry'. This, too, is the formula Brother Henri Bédel, the latest historian to write of De La Salle, makes his own in the first volume of his *Introduction to the History of the Brothers of the Christian Schools*.[4] Are we to read into this passive form ('he was offered') the effect of an external influence brought to bear on the plan of young John Baptist? It would be quite in keeping with the bourgeois spirit of the times to try to draw profit for the whole family from the advancement of one of its members. This is without casting any doubt whatsoever, in this case certainly, on the sincerity of the religious sentiments of the father. Yves Poutet observes that those of Louis de La Salle's male children who reached the age of reason while he was still alive all became priests while the others followed the usual path of marriage. He sees in that unquestionable proof of the ardent faith of the parents and of the profound education they inculcated in their children. So we can allow Maillefer to speak of 'setting up'[5] and Blain to conclude triumphantly, 'thus John Baptist was now in an important position'.[6]

On 17 March 1668, De La Salle took minor orders in Rheims. Maillefer tells us that 'He then left for Paris for the Sorbonne to study those things suitable for a person in the ecclesiastical state, and to take there his licentiate and doctorate. Louis de La Salle, his father, always anxious to give him as excellent a training as he could for the priesthood, arranged for him to stay at the Seminary of Saint Sulpice. He arrived there in the month of October 1670, at the age of nineteen years'.[7] For Blain, the seminary was 'a school of pure virtue'.[8] 'In this school ... he was taught by the most accomplished ecclesiastics'.[9] For Yves Poutet it was ' the most upper-crust seminary in the capital ... There, in fact, were prepared parish priests for the large towns, vicars general, seminary professors, even bishops'.[10]

This choice reveals in the father a constant care to procure for his eldest son the best formation then available. Also showing through is the intention of putting him in a position of assuring, if he so wished, a sound and brilliant career. Why should the interests of heaven not coincide with those of earth?

A vocation put on hold

On different occasions the deaths of loved ones occurred in the life of John Baptist de La Salle and deflected him from the course he intended to follow. The death of his mother on 19 July 1671, and especially that of his father on 9 April 1672, recalled him to Rheims. Although he was still legally a minor, he had to assume the guardianship of his brothers and sisters. Blain comments sombrely, 'All his own plans were disrupted'.[11]

How was he to reconcile his preparation for the priesthood with managing a complicated patrimony and the care and education of four brothers and two sisters? How was this to be done, even remembering that Rose Marie had already joined the monastery of Saint Étienne-des-Dames in Rheims, and that his grandmother, Pierrette Lespagnol, for practical reasons, had taken into her home Marie, the eldest, who was 18, and Jean-Remy, the youngest, who was only two. So John Baptist, the eldest brother, came to the family home in rue Sainte Marguerite, to live with Jacques-Joseph (13), Jean-Louis, his godson (8), and Pierre (6).

John Baptist was then only 21 years of age. Determined, according to the spirit of Saint Sulpice, not to act except under obedience, he sought out a new father and found him in the person of Nicholas Roland, his cousin, nine years older than himself. Nicholas was also a canon and theologian of the Rheims cathedral.

On his advice John Baptist resumed evening courses in theology. Following on from this, and 'with the option of choosing a career in the world rather than in the clerical state, he was happy to have another chance to reaffirm his prior decision', Blain tells us,[12] and on 11 June 1672, he went off to Cambrai, there to receive the sub-diaconate.

2. A pastoral vocation

A concern for family

For four years from 1672 to 1676 John Baptist de La Salle reconciled his activities as a canon with his family obligations. Having become for his brothers a substitute father and mother, he was about to live with them an exceptional educative relationship, which would influence him as well, marking him in a definite manner. He would remember it later on when he wished to form in his own spirit the schoolmasters whom he already called 'Brothers', and who, in relation to their pupils, would be in a position very like his own, that of 'elder brothers' (the expression is Blain's), substituting for parents.[13]

He will later tell his Brothers:

> You should look upon the children whom you are charged to teach as poor, abandoned orphans. In fact, though the majority of them do have a father here on earth, they are still as if they had none and are abandoned to themselves for the salvation of their souls. This is the reason God places them as if under your guardianship. He looks on them with compassion and takes care of them as being their protector, their support and their father, and it is to you he entrusts this care.[14]

He wants to do more

Blain remarks that Nicholas Roland was 'involved in many good works, that he did not limit himself to being present in the choir nor to the minimum duties of a canon'.[15] 'Seeing John Baptist filled with grace and the Holy Spirit and endowed with the talents needed in governing souls along with the strength and courage required in the most difficult undertakings, his director thought that a parish would be a more appropriate position for him than a canon's stall and that as a parish priest he would be more useful to the Church.'[16] John Baptist agreed to renounce his canonry and become parish priest of Saint-Pierre-le-Vieil. An agreement to this effect was drawn up on 20 January 1676 but the family went to the archbishop asking him to refuse his consent. For his part, on 2 March following, the parish priest of the coveted parish, standing back from the obligation of residing in Rheims, stood down and retired to Châlons.

The attempt failed. But it had led John Baptist to consider his vocation from another angle. Nicholas Roland had awakened a pastoral sense in him. He knew that from now on he must become involved in this area, but he did not yet know to what extent and especially in what way. If it was undoubtedly neither as a canon nor as a parish priest, then, as what? While awaiting a significant sign from God he remained open and available.

He attains his majority

On 30 April 1676, he attained his majority at the age of 25. Is there a link to be seen between this event and the authorisation he sought on the preceding 10 March to be discharged from his guardianship? It is a paradoxical situation. Having received and accepted the duties while he was juridically ineligible because he was still a minor, now that he fulfilled the conditions he put the responsibility aside.

The reason given is his preparation for the priesthood. He received the diaconate in Paris on 21 March,[17] and from that time on did not wish to have on his mind or in his heart any other concern than to follow the divine will to a service in the Church which he saw as more apostolic, but without being able at this stage to discern its concrete implications. He already applied the rule which, within a few years, he would impose on himself following his reading of the Jesuit Haineufve: 'It is a good rule to be less anxious to know what we are to do than to do perfectly what we do know' (*Rules I have imposed upon myself*, no. 14). In the *Collection* he would counsel the Brothers to do the same, 'for in doing it as well as you know how, you deserve to learn and understand what you would not otherwise know'.[18]

He is ordained

On 9 April 1678, Holy Saturday, John Baptist was ordained priest in Rheims Cathedral. The next day he celebrated his first Mass.

On 27 April, Canon Nicholas Roland, his spiritual director and close friend, died. It could be thought that his decease would bring to an end the decisive role he had played until then in the vocation of John Baptist. The opposite was the case. Roland had named him as executor of his will, confiding to him a double task. He was to see to the legal establishment of the school Roland had started at the institution for orphans and to obtain letters patent for the Sisters of the Child Jesus which Roland had founded on 27 December 1670, for the Christian education of girls. Legal recognition was gained on 11 August 1678, and the letters patent were signed in February 1679.

So each morning John Baptist went and celebrated Mass in the chapel of the Sisters in the rue du Barbâtre where they still live. It was there that Adrien Nyel introduced himself to John Baptist somewhere between 9 and 15 March 1679.

Adrien Nyel

Adrien Nyel was 58 years of age. For the previous 22 years he was contracted to the Office for the Poor at the General Hospital in Rouen. In this capacity he worked with the children held there and was in charge of the rudimentary education they received as well as of the labour they had to perform. 'It was likewise part of his task to teach them catechism.'[19]

Being most zealous for the Christian education of poor children, he helped with the opening of free schools for boys as well as girls in Rouen and its suburbs. Thus he came into contact with the Sisters of Providence, founded in Rouen by Father Barré in 1666. Two of them, Françoise Duval and Anne le Coeur, later went to Rheims at the request of Nicholas Roland and became the first two Sisters of the Child Jesus in 1670. Adrien Nyel also came in contact with generous rich families, among whom were M. and Mme Maillefer, who supported the charity schools of Rouen with their subsidies. Mme Maillefer who hailed from Rheims happened to be a relative of John Baptist de La Salle. The world is small but the plans of Providence are limitless.

Having become a widow and inherited a fortune from her spouse, and wishing to bring to the city of her birth the advantages she had helped to provide for her adopted city, Jeanne Maillefer made an agreement with Nicholas Roland to finance schools for boys such as already existed for girls in Rheims. Roland's death put this plan in abeyance but she did not give it up and negotiated with the Rouen Office for the Poor to grant leave to Adrien Nyel for a few years. She sent him to Rheims as the bearer of two letters, one for the Mother Superior of the Sisters of the Child Jesus, and the other for her cousin, John Baptist de La Salle.

Later on, De La Salle would confess in the *Memoir of the Beginnings*, 'Prior to this [Mme de Croyère's request for a school] I had never given them a thought. The suggestion, of course, had been made to me before. Several of Canon Roland's friends had tried to hint to me to become involved, but the proposal had never made any impression on my mind, and I had never considered carrying it out'.[20]

However, he would lend a hand in the undertaking and advised sheltering under the authority of the parish priests. So it was that schools opened in the parish of Saint Maurice on 15 April 1679, and in the parish of Saint James on the following 2 October. 'As yet he had nothing directly to do with the two schools that had been established other than what his charity inspired him to do for all sorts of good works … He let Nyel take full charge of the teachers.'[21] Maillefer adds, 'But despite the latter's piety he was not as careful or as farsighted as he should have been. Nyel's only thought was to open new schools without making the effort to solidify those he had already started'.[22]

De La Salle becomes involved

John Baptist made up for the deficiencies. At the beginning of December 1679 he leased a house for a year and a half not far from his own residence. At Christmas he installed the teachers there, five at first then seven. Each day he had their meals taken to them from his own kitchen. Above all he gave them some regulations, 'in the first place for retiring, second for prayer and third for Mass and taking their meals'.[23] Nyel rejoiced in this. Busy as he was with his classes, and on the look-out for a third opening, he 'was absent a lot'[24] abandoning the teachers to their 'own whims'.[25]

John Baptist resolved to substitute himself for Nyel in the teachers' regard in the same way as he was his father's substitute for his brothers, and the substitute of Canon Roland in regard to the Sisters of the Child Jesus. From 14 to 20 April 1680, for Holy Week, he took the teachers into his own house from morning prayer until night prayer, and from 24 June he welcomed them for meals. He thought that in this way they would acquire more polite manners and habits of piety.

That same year, he was awarded the Doctor's cap for his theological studies, and from 28 July onwards took up again the guardianship of his brothers. In October a third school opened in the parish of Saint Symphorian. During the winter he lost his way in the snow and fell into a deep hole. At sunrise he eventually climbed out, at the price of 'a hernia which inconvenienced him for the rest of his life'.[26] 'The event gave him matter for deep meditations on God's protection which he had enjoyed and new motives for serving God with greater fervour. He was so touched by this consideration that he never spoke of the incident except with great expressions of gratitude.'[27]

De La Salle lodges the teachers in his own home

In 1681 the teachers again spent Holy Week on retreat in John Baptist's home. From 24 June onwards, relinquishing the lease on their house, he lodged them in his own. Having them together with his own brothers 'was bound to cause a good deal of excitement and much talk in the city and to provoke complaints and loud outcries from the De La Salle family'.[28] In July his guardianship was revoked. His godson, Jean-Louis (17), refused to leave him. But Pierre, aged 15, was entrusted to his aunt Marie, and Jean-Remy, aged 11, was placed as a boarder with the Augustinians of Senlis, contrary to the wishes of John Baptist. At the same time, at the end of an action brought against him at the start of the year by his brother-in-law for the sharing of the inheritance, he was compelled to auction off the moveable and immoveable assets of the family patrimony. A year later the sale became effective for the residence in rue Sainte-Marguerite. He had moved into this house at the age of 12, his parents had died there and he was still living in it.

Things continued to blossom

Requests for new schools came to him from neighbouring towns. Anxious to stay in Rheims where his duties as canon retained him, he begged Adrien Nyel to take responsibility for them. So the latter left him at Christmas. It would be four years before they would be together again.

So now John Baptist de La Salle was alone with the teachers and in charge of them. Later, in the M*emoir of the Beginnings*, he would confide, 'I had thought that the care which I took of the schools and of the teachers would only be external, something that would not involve me any further than to provide for their subsistence and to see to it that they carried out their duties with piety and assiduity'.[29]

The first part of this program, providing for their upkeep, certainly implied only an 'external' preoccupation. But John Baptist had had ample time, over more than two years, to realize that it was not the same for the second part and that the reality did not come up to his expectations. M. Nyel's recruits, people without means and ready to accept any occupation whatsoever in order to survive, displayed serious deficiencies as much in the classroom as in their personal lives. To make them worthy of their mission they needed a formation that did not stop at the professional level but reached the man and the Christian in each of them.

Of course, because the pupils were themselves uncouth, they would scarcely take offence at the coarseness of the teachers. But this situation could have hardly any other result than to lock the children in and confirm them in their own grossness. How could they be cured of the bad habits they had acquired on the streets without the teachers giving proof of an upright and religious bearing?

That is why John Baptist de La Salle thought that he should not be satisfied with introducing an adapted methodology into his classes. He sought, primarily, to put at their head men whose good example shone out. To mould them to his wishes he brought them together under one roof, mapped out regulations which controlled them from morning till night and gradually educated them. In addition, to instil unity of mind in them, he went so far as to advise them all to take the one confessor, who was to be the parish priest of Saint Symphorian.

It soon became clear that 'the majority of the teachers who had lived with M. Nyel in the house rented for them … could not accommodate themselves for long to so restrained and secluded a life as that to which the fervent canon urged them in his own house. This was the reason that, desirous of a freer and more independent life, they withdrew shortly afterwards. And he was even obliged to dismiss some who, although they were pious enough, had neither talent nor vocation for the schools'.[30]

These defections, pointed out also by Blain recounting the same circumstances, are a negative picture of the ideal Saint John Baptist de La Salle had for the teachers from the beginning. It consisted of a close combination of pedagogical qualities and Christian virtues. In his thinking, the school could not limit itself to endowing the child solely with intellectual acquirements—reading, writing, arithmetic and even knowledge of religion. The school should offer to the pupils a complete education which would permit them as adults to live honourably in society.

Is there any need to go further and get to the origins of the explanation? From his earliest years De La Salle was used to giving alms to beggars, and as a canon in charge of the charitable works of the church of Rheims he was aware for a long time of the existence of poverty. He accepted it as a social evil and as inevitable because it was structural. 'The poor you have always with you' (Matthew 26:11). He therefore went along with the religious attitude which asked the poor to put up with their indigence with resignation, and at the same time called on the rich to help them generously.

But in contact with the pupils and teachers he became aware of a vastly more serious reality. Destitution kept its victims in a situation which distanced them from salvation when it did not directly put them in danger. As a Christian and a priest, he could not resign himself to this. So it must be asked if, from that point, he allocated to the school the objective to which he would come back so insistently throughout his writings on diverse subjects. The objective of his schools was to make the pupils good Christians.

New young people present themselves

The story continues: 'After the first six months of the teachers living with him, that is after 24 June 1681 and at the beginning of the year 1682, new subjects applied to him. These had some talent for school and some piety as well as being disposed to live in community',[31] as Blain would say 'to become true disciples of M. De La Salle'.[32] John Baptist would be demanding in a different way from M. Nyel. 'And it was then that a true form of community began to be seen in the house.'[33]

In the light of this, John Baptist de La Salle decided to take the plunge. In rue Neuve he rented two houses side by side and moved in with his brother Jean-Louis, ten teachers and three ecclesiastics he had taken in. The following month the residence in rue Sainte-Marguerite was sold. John Baptist could have continued to live there by renting it. So it was not its sale that forced him to leave it but the deliberate choice to settle in at last with the teachers, as he felt God was asking him to do.

How many other saints, before and after him, began their quest for God by the decisive step of leaving their home! John Baptist's exodus, having left to live with those he destined to run schools, presents two aspects, one community and the other pastoral. These two characteristics of his work would remain as inseparable as the two faces of a single coin. There would be no community activity that would not be, at the same time, pastoral, and no pastoral activity that would not also have a community perspective.

Since the failure of the plan to become a parish priest — a happy failure as it proved — he was searching for a more pastoral service to the Church than the canonry. As long as the work of the schools seemed to him, in his own words, 'a duty of pure charity',[34] he restricted himself to devoting to it only an 'external care'.[35] If at this point he interiorized the involvement he brought to it, it was because he grasped that it opened up for him a choice opportunity for displaying the apostolic zeal awakened in his heart by Roland.

Events move rapidly

From then on things moved quickly. A fourth school was opened in Rethel on 26 February, a fifth opened in Guise on 26 June and a sixth at Château-Porcien on the 30th of the same month. A seventh would open in Laon in November. Bernard comments, 'By the end of 1682 it was plain to M. De La Salle that God was calling him to care for the schools'.[36] Blain puts it in his own way: 'Finally, after much reflection in God's presence, after many prayers and consultations, it seemed evident to him "towards the end of the year 1682" as he himself writes, that God was calling him to take charge of the schools'.[37]

The teachers asked De La Salle to be their confessor. He hesitated, then complied with their wishes. He clarified and detailed the regulations of the house. Starting in the month of September they adopted the daily exercises.

Finally they chose a name for themselves:

> That of 'Brothers' was the one that fitted them best, so they chose it, giving up the name of 'Schoolmasters' to those who practise this profession for gain … This name teaches them how excellent is the duty they have assumed, the dignity of their state, and the holiness proper to their profession. It tells them that as Brothers they owe each other mutual proofs of tender but spiritual friendship; and that considering themselves as the elder brothers of the children who come to be taught by them, they should exercise this ministry of charity with truly loving hearts.[38]

Lasallian texts

Selected texts illustrating the background of the society in which the young were far from salvation and how De La Salle's writings helped the first Lasallian educators confront this challenge.

Social conditions of the times

We see that these children run like wild asses during the procession, sometimes four, six, ten or twelve together, shouting, screaming and fighting one another, parish against parish, using sticks, stones and other instruments. This comes about through the neglect of parents and school masters (Jacques de Batencour, *L'escole Paroissiale*, 1654).

Badly brought up young people usually fall into laziness. Whence it follows that they do nothing but run about the streets aimlessly; that you see groups of them at street corners where they engage mostly in loose talk. They become intractable, dissolute, gamblers, blasphemers and quarrelsome. They give themselves up to drunkenness, debauchery, thieving and robbery. Finally they become the most depraved and factious of the commonwealth. Being corrupt members they would spoil the rest if the tormentor's whip, the prince's galleys and the gallows of justice did not rid the earth of these venomous serpents who infect society (Charles Démia, *Remonstrances*, 1666).

From whence, do you imagine, come disorders and jealousy in the home, the many odious places in the city, the many abandoned children in the Poor House, and the many public family break-ups, except from the lack of sufficient care in the education of girls? They have been left in ignorance, then they have fallen into idleness, then into lying, unruliness, inconstancy and finally into destitution, which is the commonest reef on which the modesty of this sex is wrecked (Charles Démia, *Remonstrances*, 1666).

These poor children of both sexes, it seems, receive the life of the body only to lose that of their souls. They find in their family homes only pernicious examples and instruction solely in evil. These vagrant children roam the streets. They know only how to play, get up to mischief, play malicious tricks, tease, romp about, fight and squabble. These children go to church only to cause trouble, turmoil and bad example. Or they are there like animals knowing neither where they are nor what they come there to do. They know not what they owe to the One in whose sight they laugh, punch and abuse one another. While growing up these children use obscene language, become drunkards and professional libertines. On replacing their fathers they carry on the generation of unfaithful and irreligious men who are without the use of reason … Usually the first use they make of their reason is to lose their innocence. Seemingly this great treasure is such a burden to them that they hasten to rid themselves of it. As they do not know its value nor the consequences, they sacrifice it for trifles …Thus these children familiarized with vice and more or less looking upon it as normal no longer perceive its evil and, with age, lose any horror of it. While still young they are experienced libertines, and, as youths, they are real scoundrels and old in the ways of impiety. They give scandal and are often the scourge of their neighbourhood (J. B. Blain, *The life of M. John Baptist de La Salle*, 1733).[39]

The children who come to you either have not had any instruction, or have been taught the wrong things, or, if they have received some good lessons, bad companions or their own bad habits have prevented them from benefiting (*Meditations*, 37, 2).

In a society which does not allow parents to exercise their rightful educational roles the Brother takes the place of parents and pastors.

… the working class and the poor being usually little instructed, and being occupied all day in gaining a livelihood for themselves and their families, cannot give their children the needed instruction or a suitable Christian education. Therefore there need to be other persons taking the place of fathers and mothers to give the children as much instruction as they need in the mysteries of religion and the principles of the Christian life (Rule of 1705, 1, 4).

God intervenes.

It is characteristic of the providence of God and of his vigilance over human conduct to substitute for fathers and mothers persons who have enough knowledge and zeal to bring children to the knowledge of God and his mysteries. According to the grace of Jesus Christ, that God has given to them, they are like good architects who give all possible care and attention to lay the foundation of religion and Christian piety in the hearts of these children, a great number of whom would otherwise be abandoned (*MTR*, 193, 2).

The Brother should act like the Father.

… fulfil well the service that he himself gave you. For he has made you the guardians and guides of children who belong to him, over whom he has acquired the right of father not only by creation but also by holy baptism, whereby they are all consecrated to him (*MTR*, 205, 1).

De La Salle believed that the Brothers have the task of making up for the deficiencies of families and society.

God has given you no less an honour than he gave Saint Joachim by placing you in the work you have, since he has destined you to be the spiritual fathers of the children whom you instruct. If this saint was chosen to be the father of the Most Blessed Virgin, you have been destined by God to produce children for Jesus Christ, and even to produce and engender Jesus Christ himself in their hearts (*Meditations*, 157, 1).

You should look upon the children whom you are charged to teach as poor, abandoned orphans. In fact, though the majority of them do have a father here on earth, they are still as if they had none and are abandoned to themselves for the salvation of their souls. This is the reason God places them as if under your guardianship.

He looks on them with compassion and takes care of them as being their protector, their support and their father, and it is to you he entrusts their care. This God of goodness places them in your hands and undertakes to give them everything you ask of him for them: piety, self-control, reserve, purity, the avoidance of companions who could be dangerous to them. And because God knows that of yourself you have neither enough virtue nor enough ability to give all these things to the children he has entrusted to you, he wants you to ask him for these blessings for them frequently, fervently, and insistently. In this way, thanks to your care, nothing will be lacking to them that they need for their salvation (*Meditations*, 37, 3).

The Brothers take the place of pastors.

For in these matters you are taking the place of the pastors of the Church and their fathers and mothers (Meditations, 61, 3).

You are substitutes for their fathers and mothers and their pastors (*MTR*, 203, 3).

They take the place of priests and even of bishops.

You are in a work that by its ministry resembles that of priests more than it does any other work (Meditations, 186, 2).

Is not this the function of a Bishop, to oppose vice and to maintain the faith in its vigour and strength? This is also what you cannot dispense yourself from doing, if you wish to fulfil your ministry, to prevent your students from abandoning themselves to vice and dissolute conduct and impress firmly and solidly on their minds the truths of our faith, which are the foundations of our religion (*Meditations*, 132, 3).

From all this comes the importance of the Lasallian ministry in the Church.

You must, then, look upon your work as one of the most important and most necessary services in the Church, one which has been entrusted to you by pastors, by fathers and mothers (*MTR*, 199, 1).

And the duties which flow from it for the Brother.

Do you have these sentiments of charity and tenderness towards the poor children whom you have to educate? Do you take advantage of their affection for you to lead them to God? If you have for them the firmness of a father to restrain and withdraw them from misbehaviour, you must also have for them the tenderness of a mother to draw them to you, and to do for them all the good that depends on you (*Meditations*, 101, 3).

God will punish you for your neglect [in not punishing the faults of your students]. Since you are the substitutes for their fathers and mothers, you are obliged to keep watch over these children as the one who is accountable for their souls (*MTR*, 203, 3).

You have committed yourselves to God in the place of those whom you instruct. By taking upon yourselves the responsibility for their souls, you have, so to speak, offered to him soul for soul. Have you sometimes reflected on the commitment you have made (to be responsible for those whom God has entrusted to you), in order to be faithful to it? Do you have as much care for their salvation as you have for your own? You should not only take all possible care of them, but consecrate your life and yourselves entirely to procure salvation for them (*Meditations*, 137, 3).

Chapter 2

The House

The Mother House

The foundation date for the Institute is given as 24 June 1682. The dwelling in rue Neuve should be regarded as the Mother-House (*Maison-Mère*), a title ascribed to the place where a religious congregation is first established. Common usage of the word in French connects it with business law, which designates the 'Mother-house' as the head office of a corporation as opposed to its branch offices. Today the name 'Mother House' is given to the centre of the Institute in Rome where the Superior-General resides and from where its general business activity is conducted. The cluster of buildings where the little group was first installed is now 27 rue Gambetta. At first rented, the buildings were purchased in 1700, 'aided by a few charitable persons in the city'.[1]

The property had an entrance on the rue Neuve and another in the Cour du Leu which opened onto the rue de Contrai. The rear of the enclosure was on the site of the present Technical High School (Lycée) of Saint John Baptist de La Salle. The Founder spent only six years in this house about which Blain fittingly remarks, 'No doubt God destined it to be the cradle of his Institute. It was there in fact that the Institute began'.[2]

The customs of the house

The manner in which De La Salle lived there with his disciples is learned from *The Practice of the Daily Timetable* which governed daily living.[3] This was not a rule of life or the Religious Rule. It was simply a timetable, which indicated what was to be done at different times of the day, on Sundays,

Feast Days or holidays, and on special occasions notably when Brothers die. The timetable was strictly practical in its scope.

The manuscript copy, kept in the Institute Archives, bears the date of 9 March 1713. But it 'appears to preserve in many places a form of wording which is much older, dating back probably to the first years of the Community … We are of the opinion that this daily time-table was part of the primitive Rule — where we see outlined, for the use of each school community, the general principles applicable to daily living'.[4]

Our interest is aroused when we read, for example: 'The brothers shall at all times rise at half past four o'clock. The bell-ringer must rise when the alarm rings a quarter of an hour at the latest before the half hour. He rings the bell on the last note of the clock at 4.30 am exactly. Then he goes and knocks on the dormitory doors, saying while knocking "Live Jesus in our hearts" to which those within the dormitory reply "Forever". This is the Community signal'.[5]

Or again we read: 'At half past eight o'clock evening prayer shall be recited in the Chapel after which the Brothers shall remain a short time in Recollection until the Brother Director says "Live Jesus in our hearts", and the Brothers reply "Forever". Then they go to the dormitory and at nine o'clock the bell shall be tolled thirty times to give warning that everyone has to withdraw to the dormitories in order to be in bed by 9.15. From that time it is not permitted to speak even to the Superior until after mental prayer next morning'.[6]

These passages give us an impression of austerity. The layout of the rooms is spartan and arranged solely to fit the need of a pious and strict style of community living: an oratory where the Blessed Sacrament is not reserved; not a huge dormitory but rather rooms that several Brothers share; a refectory where meals are taken in silence with reading at table; a room for community exercises, where the Brothers gather for spiritual reading, study of catechism, and preparation for class. They go to the parish church at a quarter past seven and assist at Holy Mass, which is the first that can be attended after six o'clock.[7] Similarly, 'The Brothers who teach school away from the house leave the oratory and the house without stopping anywhere and reciting the rosary going and coming in the morning and after mid-day'.[8] There is an atmosphere of silence and recollection, all the exercises are performed in common, a bell summons the Brothers to the exercises, which begin and end with prayer. 'For each exercise, the bell shall be tolled thirty times neither more nor less and after ringing, thirty strokes shall be sounded for mental prayer, Holy Mass, for lunch, for the evening meal, for evening prayer.'[9] Nothing capricious then marked this life totally dedicated to work, prayer, and poverty throughout days punctuated by the 'Live Jesus in our hearts' which itself echoes Sulpician devotion of which we find very similar formulas used by Father Nicolas Barré, Louis-Marie Grignion de Montfort, John Eudes and other spiritual writers of the period.

The men who formed the community

What seemed most unusual, under the circumstances, was the fact that the men who lived this life more suited to the most austere of monasteries and who already bore the name of Brothers, were not religious, and had not entered this house intending to become such, and perceived as yet nothing in the way of life they were leading which could lead to their becoming such. Nor did they envisage the priesthood. Some of their number, who before becoming acquainted with John Baptist De La Salle, had engaged in clerical studies, 'gave up their studies and came to join him ... convinced that they would be accomplished enough when they had learned to know Christian Doctrine and to practise it to the letter. They felt that even though they were neither priests nor clerics, they could fulfil this mission of teaching, which is most necessary and most useful for the poor and most sanctifying for those who undertake it with zeal and humility. They generously gave up the idea of receiving sacred orders and the worldly hopes they might have entertained in a more prestigious calling than that of a school master'.[10]

So these were laymen—ordinary laymen. For the majority of them, life appeared until such time as their meeting with a man of God made them realize that there were others in greater distress: those children whose parents 'obliged to look for work outside their homes have to abandon the children to themselves'.[11] Finding, as De La Salle did, that the school provided a remedy for the distress of these 'orphans', they were willing to live with him in community to engage in mutual training and support with a view to helping their pupils become Christians in accord with Gospel teaching. For the laymen, of course, there was no question of marriage. De La Salle never in any of his writings referred to them as 'celibates', it was undoubtedly because the word did not find its way into the French language until 1711, eight years before his death; however, nor did he use the word 'celibacy' which had been in existence from 1549 to describe the state of the unmarried.

He preferred to say, 'those who live in the Communities'. Most certainly the concept of community (in his time the word was regularly used to designate a religious community) included the notion of celibacy, but it was used more widely to include many other values.

He who at one time planned to engage in an individual priestly apostolate now realized that his pastoral work was to be with laymen living in the community. He would later write in the *Memoir on the Habit* that 'there are few priests in most town parishes, often there is only one parish priest, or at most, one curate with him.'[12]

At a time when, following the impetus of the Council of Trent, societies of priests were springing up and multiplying, John Baptist De La Salle was proving an innovator in establishing a society of laymen. For this reason, it is interesting to note that he used the word 'community' to describe his society.

We encounter the word 'community' for the first time in a letter dated 20 June 1682, four days before the beginnings in rue Neuve. It is the oldest of his letters we have preserved. Replying to the Mayor and Alderman of Chateau-Porcien who wanted to provide their town with a Christian school and so were requesting him to send Brothers, he wrote, 'It would be very wrong of me, gentlemen, not to send you schoolmasters from our community'. It is worth noting that De La Salle makes this statement without making any suggestion of religious life. Later on he will use the words 'Society' or 'Institute' with the same understanding. The plan he had in mind was far too new in the Church's thinking for the word 'community' to be a specific description. It was necessary therefore for him to take a word already in existence, even if he had to modify its established meaning in order to meet his need. So to describe what today we call a local community, he retained the word 'house' (*maison*).

Lasallian texts

School teachers who are neither priests nor married men.

For persons that would be employed to take charge of schools (to be schoolteachers), it must be stated, that neither priests nor married men should be sought because the former would be distracted by their priestly duties from the application needed in their employment, or by the parish priests who would not be slow to call on them to assist in parish work, or by benefices (lucrative positions) which, coming their way, would mean their place as teachers would become vacant. The married men would likewise be diverted from their attention to their teaching tasks by their domestic duties and by their mercenary spirit (the worries of a paid job) which usually motivates them and since it would be necessary for the proper performance of their teaching duties to require them sometimes to change their place of dwelling, either because of their slackness or bad habits they had contracted or for any other important reasons, such a change would be all the more difficult when family and social ties had become numerous. It would be necessary, then, to ask bishops to require the majority of seminarians, especially those in minor orders, to work in the schools as a sort of novitiate for the priesthood, for which they would not normally be accepted, until they had worthily acquitted themselves of caring for the young people entrusted to their care … Unmarried persons could also be recruited, who would be expected to continue living in that state as long as they were engaged in teaching. After discharging their teaching tasks in praiseworthy fashion these persons could with quite accurate judgment be told to 'go up higher ' unless of course they wanted to continue in the kind of life they had embraced. As the scope and excellence of the role of schoolteacher rightly demands persons who are free of marriage ties and ready to devote themselves entirely to their work, it would seem celibacy is required for the work to flourish (Charles Démia, *Important advice for setting up a Teacher Training Establishment*, 1688).

Those who compose this community are all laymen, without classical studies and of little culture. Providence permitted that some of those who applied, who had received the tonsure or who had begun their humanities failed to remain. Youths who have started their humanities, however, will not be refused, but they will be received only on condition that they give up the study of the classics,

1. because in the first place, this will not be necessary for them;
2. because it might subsequently become an enticement for them to leave their state;
3. because the community exercises and the occupation of teaching require one's whole attention.[13]

De La Salle's first letter

To the Mayor and Councillors of Chateau-Porcien
Reims June 20 1682

Gentlemen,

Even were I to take but little interest in what concerns the glory of God, I would indeed be quite insensitive not to be moved by the urgent pleas of your Reverend Dean and by the courteous tone of the letter with which you have honoured me today. It would be wrong of me, Gentlemen, not to send you school teachers from our community, in view of the enthusiasm and zeal you show for the Christian education and instruction of your children. So please be assured that nothing is dearer to my heart than to support your good intentions in this matter. By this Saturday I will send you two school-teachers with whom I trust you will be satisfied, to open classes the day following the feast of Saint Peter. I assure you that I am very much obliged to you for your courteous remarks.

I beg you, gentlemen, to believe that, with respect and in Our Lord, I am your very humble and obedient servant,
De La Salle, Priest, Canon of Rheims[14]

It was a Canon of Rheims Cathedral who wrote to the Mayor and councillors of the town, which they wished to endow with a Christian school. Chateau-Porcien was the capital of a territory acquired by the Duke of Mazarin. It is located about ten miles from Rethel where in March 1682 Adrian Nyel had opened a school. John Baptist De La Salle was evidently aware of his role as Superior. He had a full understanding of the purpose of his institute namely 'the instruction and Christian education of children'. These two terms will appear again in the First Rule (Chapters 1 and 4) This was the first occasion that John Baptist De La Salle used the word 'community' to describe his group of teachers. He used it again in the first article of the *Practices of the Daily Timetable*: 'He goes and knocks on the doors of the dormitory, and says while knocking 'Live Jesus in our hearts' and those within reply 'Forever'. This is the signal of the Community'.[15]

We must refrain from giving to this word 'Community' the notion of a religious community.

Chapter 3

The poverty of
the Apostle

Contestation by the Brothers

In September 1682, at the opening of classes, deep anxiety began to gnaw at
the Brothers concerning their future. Would the enterprise on which they
had entered endure? What could they expect if it came to an end? After the
first burst of generosity, this doubt acted like a brake, a fear which spread like
a contagion all the more dangerous in that it was fed by memories of the
past, a past still alive and very much present to their memory.

The work, in fact, depended on the generosity of benefactors; if this
dried up, the work ceased. Doubtless, they could count on the zealous Canon
to make up from his own resources any financial gap which would arise. 'But
he may die tomorrow; and once he is gone what will become of the schools
he, is supporting? What will become of the Masters whom he provides for
and whose father he is? Where can we go? What can we do when M. De La
Salle is longer with us?'[1]

De La Salle (who was at this time only 31) was aware of the concern of
his followers. Convinced that God never fails us, he strove to restore their
confidence by a fervent address which Maillefer and Blain cite 'Men of little
faith, do you insist on setting restrictions on God's Providence ? ... If He has
care of the grass and the lilies of the field, as Himself says, and the birds and
the other animals even if they have, neither resources, income, cellar, nor
granaries, how much more will He provide for you who are devoted entirely

to His service?'[2] The Brothers' response was brutally sincere: 'You have everything, you are secure, you have money, you still have your canonry. All these things will save you from the wretchedness into which we shall fall if the schools should fail'.[3] De La Salle saw the force of this argument and stated that they were right in bringing it up with him. From this moment he realized that the best way to convince them of his perfect disinterestedness was to give away all he possessed and become exactly like them.[4]

Père Barré's advice

De la Salle at first thought of using his personal fortune to fund the schools. Since he had made it a rule never to undertake anything without prayer and consultation, he had himself locked in the Basilica of Saint-Rémy for several nights to ask enlightenment of God. At the same time he had recourse to the counsels of Père Barré, whose advice he had already sought in 1680 before he brought the schoolmasters into his family home.

This religious, who for his own schools in Rouen had wished for no other funding than the help of God and, for the Sisters of Providence, so well named, no other spirituality than total surrender into the hands of the heavenly Father, disapproved of the idea. The advice given him is recounted by Maillefer and Blain in practically the same terms: '"Foxes have holes, the birds of the sky have their nests, but the Son of Man has nowhere to rest his head"' (Matthew 8: 20). This is how Père Barré commented on these words: 'The foxes are the children of the world who are attached to riches. The birds of the air are religious, who have their monasteries, but those who, like you, are destined to instruct and catechize the poor ought to have no more of this world's goods than the Son of Man. Not only should you give away everything you own, but you ought to resign your canonry and renounce everything that would be able to distract you from procuring the glory of God'.[5]

Let us leave to Père Barré the responsibility for his exegesis. Nonetheless his reading of the gospel merits our reflection. The contrast he draws between the schoolmasters and, on the one hand, the simple faithful and, on the other, religious is valid in his thought only from the viewpoint of the way wealth is used. Christians living in the world may make use of wealth freely in the measure of its availability: religious renounce wealth by setting themselves apart from it. As to the schoolmasters, who 'have no other resource on earth than that of the Son of Man', they seek above all the King-dom of Heaven in themselves and in the hearts of their pupils, while waiting that all other things be given them in abundance. The lesson is clear and it will be remembered by the one for whom it had been spelled out.

Can we go further and transfer this distinction of the manner in which evangelical poverty may be practised to that of religious life and its juridical status? Did its author wish to imply that the Brothers, though not to be con-sidered in any strict sense as religious, could be considered no longer as simple faithful. Thus they would occupy in the Church a place of their own, not yet well defined or categorized, but quite specific and not to be assimilated to any other. This would make John Baptist de La Salle an innovator not only in the domain of schooling but also an innovator in the domain of religious life.

Let us recognize that this analysis, attractive as it is, goes well beyond the thought of Père Barré and distracts us from its real implication. To the spirit of abandonment which John Baptist proposed to the Brothers—to become poor so as to imitate Christ who cherished and practised poverty—Père Barré opposed an abandonment of a pastoral type: to detach oneself from everything to give oneself in all liberty to the proclamation of the Good News. 'Provide yourselves with no gold or silver, not even with a few coppers in your purses, with no haversack for the journey or spare tunic or footwear or a staff, for the workman deserves his keep' (Matthew 10:9-10).

The reaction of De La Salle

Thus, convinced that one cannot be an apostle unless one is poor, John Baptist in the first place rid himself of his canonry. According to the testi-mony of Bernard, the steps involved took some nine or ten months[6] and reached conclusion only in August 1683. 'The joy which he then experi-enced was so great ... that he had the Brothers join him in their oratory in singing a *Te Deum*.'[7]

However,

he did not believe the sacrifice to be complete unless he gave up all he owned in favour of the poor ... His first thought was to give everything to the school Brothers, who were certainly the poor most particularly confided to his care ... Those who would have blamed his too great detachment from the goods of this world would have nothing but praise for this use of his wealth to found his Institute. He would thus provide for his Brothers and preserve them permanently from the fear of lacking the necessities of life, which had troubled them only a short time before ... On the other hand, the thought of Divine Providence, the principal motivation of all his actions, was returning repeatedly to his mind.[8]

My God, I do not know whether to endow the schools or not. It is not up to me but to you to establish and maintain a community of teachers. You alone know how to bring this about in the manner most pleasing to you. I dare not endow the schools, for I do not know your will, nor shall 1 take any steps to found our houses. If you support them they will be well supported, but if you do not they shall remain without support.[9]

Once again events provided him with an answer. The winter of 1683–84 was very severe and John Baptist began to sell his possessions to share them with the unfortunate in the form of food and clothing. Moreover, because the following winter, throughout the kingdom and particularly in Rheims, caused an even more terrible famine, he continued to lavish his help upon the deserving poor[10] as well as upon the families of the pupils of his three schools for boys and the four schools for girls of the Sisters of the Child Jesus 'until little remained of his earthly goods. On the advice of his director and some intimate friends, he did hold back a personal income of 200 livres so as not to tempt Providence.'[11]

What did this sum signify?

Bernard offers us in John Baptist's manner of acting a very revealing detail. These 200 livres were the equivalent of the annual stipend which the benefactors of the schools undertook to pay for each Brother. This sum had been calculated on the average income of a poor country parish priest. It was also the salary paid to clerics who taught in the schools opened in Lyons by Charles Démia[12] in 1667 and 1671.

In giving up his canonry, John Baptist put an end to a crucifying division which split him between two classes of duties, both sacred in his eyes: on the one side, attendance in choir and his canonical commitment; on the other, his care for the schools and the teachers. Now, 'released from a responsibility in which he felt of little use to the Church'[13], he could give himself completely to 'the work of God', consecrating to it all his time and all his strength.

Further, in keeping an annual sum of 200 livres, he put an end to everything that might still distinguish him from the Brothers. He placed himself on their level, made himself their equal, took on their standard of living and, except for his priesthood, became truly one of them. If in this way he sacrificed his canonry and his personal fortune, it was not to a religious ideal, holy as it might be, but to a real concrete pastoral community: he became poor to be a Brother. We can regret that his biographers have not in this instance, discerned the full truth of his real intention. Bernard writes, 'Thus it was that the pious servant of God despoiled himself of everything to follow Jesus Christ poor and destitute, and to be free to pursue his own sanctification and that of others.'[14] And Blain adds, 'Happy to possess God and nothing but God he could say with Saint Francis, that great lover of poverty, 'My God and my All!' If I have lost all for his sake, I find it all again in Him. He alone suffices.'[15]

One could not make a more serious mistake in the spiritual interpretation of the steps then taken by John Baptist de La Salle. By giving up all he owned, he entered more deeply and more personally on the path on which he had set out on 24 June 1682, when he moved into the Rue Neuve with the schoolmasters. In distributing his wealth to the poor, by an evangelical paradox, he afforded a surer guarantee to his work than if he had continued to use it as he had done up till then and, as he had at one time contemplated, to meet this or that need of the schools.

We can only admire the inner consistency of his approach, the fruit of his transparency, his total availability to the divine will. The more so, since his path was only beginning to open up before him and since the action he had just taken would bear fruit in later and more and more radical commitments.

His followers too advanced in an understanding of their vocation: having chosen in September 1682 to call themselves 'Brothers', in September 1684 they decided to complete the name: 'Brothers of the Christian Schools'.

Their dress, evolved in a similar manner. Dressed at first like common folk in knee-breeches and a tight-fitting dark jacket without pockets, the *rabat*, the white long-tailed collar, did not in their case constitute a distinctive sign, since at that time many men wore it without any special reason. In the course of the winter of 1683-84, they added as protection against the cold the cloak of the peasants of Champagne, a mantle the sleeves of which served no purpose; it was simply hung over the shoulders and buttoned under the chin. Finally, in September 1684, at the same time as they adopted a definitive name, they replaced the knee-length coat with a soutane without buttons, which came down to within *six pouces*, some fourteen centimetres, from the ground.

Being converted to the poor by the poor

The quotation from Matthew 6:25 addressed to the schoolmasters by John Baptist de La Salle corresponds to that from Mt 8,20 addressed by Père Barré to him: *consistency of the Word of God.*

This first appeal to personal poverty presents itself then under the sign of ministerial poverty. It was his intention to consecrate himself to the Christian education of poor children which led him to take on the formation of the schoolmasters, themselves poor; and it was his plan to form them which led him to make himself poor: *consistency of the guidance of God.*

His intention to renounce his personal fortune suggests to him at first that he use it for the establishment of the schools. Then he comes to understand that they too should be poor like himself: *consistency of ministerial poverty.*

Just as his intention of going to the poor comes through the establishment of a community vowed to their service, so too his demand for poverty will go to the building of the new-born Society as he expressed it in Meditation 176, On Saint Francis Borgia:

> …the more he felt the rigours of poverty, the happier he was, because he knew that Jesus Christ had given us the example of this virtue and that he had practised it to the highest degree from his birth. For this reason he felt that it was only right that those who wish to join Jesus most closely and who have the honour of belonging to his Company, should share in a perfect manner the love and practice he had for this virtue, which he desired to be the inseparable companion of his disciples.
>
> This was also what the saint required of all the members of his Company when he was their General. He even wished that all the houses of professed members who belonged to the Company should have no other foundation than poverty itself.
>
> Is this the sort of foundation on which you desire your community to be built? It is a sure and unfailing foundation for those whose faith is true and who are interiorly animated by the spirit of Our Lord. You cannot do better than to base your fortune on this foundation; it is the one that Jesus Christ thought to be most solid, and on which the holy Apostles began to build the edifice of the Church.

So too in the formula of vows of 1691

Exactly, step by step, as his enterprise becomes conscious of itself, it assumed institutional form. Thus it was that his giving up his canonry was to bring into sharp relief the problem of who should be Superior of the Institute.

The ministerial poverty of John Baptist de La Salle

The poverty which John Baptist de La Salle wanted for himself and for his Brothers was not the fruit of an ascetical discipline, of an effort to purify oneself, to disengage oneself from the material world, even if it necessarily implies such an effort. Neither was it the object of any mystical aspiration, a means of uniting oneself to the Divinity, even if, in fact this is the foundation of all spiritual life. It is, for the members of the Institute, the consequence of a will to harmonize their own condition of life with their ministry.

The Brothers should be poor because they are sent to the poor to announce to them that poverty becomes the way of salvation provided that it is lived according to the Gospel. It is not meant then only for removing every obstacle between the poor and themselves nor through a spirit of solidarity with the poor. It is by choice, choice of a human situation which incarnates the proclaiming of the Kingdom to the poor:

— identification with Christ who became poor 'to enrich us by his poverty' (2 Corinthians 8:9);

— identification with the poor, 'the ones most disposed to profit by his teaching';[16]

— identification with the message 'Blessed are you poor, the Kingdom of God is yours' (Luke 6:20).

There is in all this a concern for consistency, human as well Christian. It is poverty which attracts and keeps the attachment of the poor. It is what makes them recognize the Brothers as ministers of God and ambassadors of Christ in their regard. It is what reveals to them that God loves them and that he comes to save them.

> Be assured that so long as you remain bound in your heart to poverty and to everything that can humble you, you will do good for souls. The angels of God will make you known and will inspire fathers and mothers to send you their children to be instructed, and by your instructions you will touch the hearts of these poor children and most of them will become true Christians. But if you do not resemble the newborn Jesus by these two outstanding virtues you will be little known and little employed, nor will you be loved and appreciated by the poor, and you will never have for them the role of saviour as it is proper for you in your work, for you will draw them to God only insofar as you resemble them and Jesus at his birth.[17]

The Brothers' poverty, then, should be recognized by their students as an evangelical value. It should say to them that to be Christian is to refuse to consider money as the supreme good; it is to give up seeking it beyond what is necessary or what is to be detrimental to justice.

Evangelical poverty needs to be seen as proclamation of the Gospel

Lasallian texts

At Darnétal in 1705

Letter to Brother Robert (No. 38)

I have received your letter, my very dear Brother, and am very happy that you have great peace of mind. I pray that God may keep you in that state.

I am also delighted that you are determined to persevere in the Institute to the end of your life, and my joy is much greater because of your desire to return to the novitiate.

This is a sign that you are really desirous of advancing in virtue. This gives me great pleasure.

You must love poverty, my very dear Brother. Although he could have been rich Our Lord was very poor. So you must imitate this divine model.

But it seems to me that you want nothing to be lacking which will give you pleasure. Well, who wouldn't be poor under those conditions? Would not the great and powerful ones of the world give up all their riches to enjoy an advantage that would make them happier than the princes and kings of the earth?

Please remember that you did not join the Institute to enjoy every comfort and satisfaction but to embrace poverty and its consequences. 1 say its consequences because there is no point in loving virtue unless you love all that comes with it and gives you the means of practising it.

You say that you are poor; how much pleasure it gives me to hear you say that! For to say you are poor is to say that you are happy. 'Happy are you who are poor,' Our Lord said to his apostles. I say the same to you.

How fortunate you are! You say you have never been so poor; so much the better. You have never had so many opportunities for practising that virtue as you do now.

In this regard I could say to you what a great Pope once said to a Jesuit who was explaining the great poverty of his community, which, he said, had never been so poor. 'So much the better for you,' he replied, 'The poorer you are the better off you will be.'

Take care while the community is being set up that you do not let yourself become negligent in the practice of the Rule.

I am, my very dear Brother,
Devotedly yours in Our Lord, De La Salle

Chapter 4

The habit does not
make the monk

1. A work taking shape

De La Salle teaches class

In 1685, five of the seven schools run by the Brothers were under the control of John Baptist de La Salle. These were the three in the parishes of Saint-Maurice, Saint Jacques and Saint-Symphorien in Rheims as well as those in Rethel and Château-Porcien. The other two in Guise and Laon were the responsibility of Adrien Nyel.

Since the move to the rue Neuve on 24 June 1682, several Brothers had already died. We may not know them all but we can note the burial of Brother Cosmé Boiserins on 24 March 1684, aged 29, and of Jean Lozart on 16 June 1685, aged 25. The work of schoolmastering weakened constitutions not sufficiently hardy, meagerly and badly nourished. The Brothers were exposed to all kinds of diseases in overcrowded classrooms in which hygiene was relative and which sometimes had no ventilation except through the doorways. Added to this were 'excessive mortifications', as Blain expressly specifies for Brother Jean François who was interred on 30 September 1685, after living in the community for only eighteen months.[1]

Maillefer comments on these bereavements:

> During these first years he lost several capable Brothers who were not easily replaced. This obliged him, because of lack of vocations, to teach school himself in Saint James' Parish. It was a matter of great surprise to see him

leave the house twice a day, clothed in the short cassock of coarse material, and wearing the mantle with flowing sleeves, and wearing the broad-brimmed hat and thick-soled shoes, going with the others to teach children to read and write, and teaching them catechism, taking them to church, and in a word obeying to the letter all that he himself had set down for the regulation of the gratuitous schools. This new sight aroused the comments of the people who see things under their external appearances only. He paid no attention to these remarks, and continued his humble duties until he received new subjects capable of taking over these responsibilities.[2]

Bernard adds,

Not only did M. de La Salle teach school in Rheims but also he did so in Paris and elsewhere.[3]

Nyel's two schools

This was the moment chosen by Adrien Nyel to move on. He was 68 years old, enfeebled and very worn out. His only goal was to go back to Rouen where he was still bound by contract to the General Hospital. He requested his release from John Baptist who, wishing him to continue with the responsibility for the two schools he had founded in Guise and Laon, refused. The parish priests who provided the stipends for the Brothers intervened and Nyel departed in October. This is how Bernard concludes the episode:

It can be said that God made use of him to start the Institute of the Brothers of the Christian Schools inasmuch as he persuaded M. De La Salle to devote himself to something he had never before considered. M. Nyel was gifted with all the good qualities that can be found in the simple layman that he was.[4]

A training college for country school masters

Most of the pastors of country parishes were after De La Salle to send a Brother to instruct the children of their parish. But he always answered that he could not oblige them for he had made it a rule never to send fewer than two together and good order required that he not depart from this rule. The pastors found a compromise. This was to choose masters themselves for their parishes, and to send them to him to train them. He could not refuse this service.[5]

His great concern was to safeguard the community life of his disciples. In his eyes community life was the guarantee of their vocation. A country school required only one teacher who could reside at the presbytery. The parish priest would ask that he perform, in a surplice, certain liturgical functions in the church to the point where he was teacher, choir master and sacristan. If this person were a Brother his ties to the community would be relaxed and he would end up by leaving it. For this reason John Baptist made it a rule to set up schools only in towns where a large number of Brothers, living in the same house, could together operate in several schools in different quarters of the town and thus support one another in their state.

But he was by no means unaware of the needs of country parishes. After several attempts, which Archbishop Le Tellier dubbed 'madness', he bought, towards the end of September 1685, a little house close to the two he already had in rue Neuve, and at Christmas time he opened his door to three pupil-teachers. Here is his own description of this first teacher training college:

> They also conduct a training school for schoolmasters destined for the rural areas in a house distinct from the community residence and which is termed a seminary. These candidates remain several years in residence until they are formed to piety and to the other necessary subjects of their apostolate; they are instructed thoroughly in chant and in reading and in penmanship; board, lodging and laundry are supplied gratis; following their training they are placed in some hamlet or village to perform the offices usually reserved to clerics. As soon as they are placed they sever all connection with the society except those of goodwill and gratitude: they are permitted to return, however, to make retreats at the seminary.[6]

Very quickly their numbers increased.

The First Assembly of the Brotherhood

The following year, 1686, judging it necessary to strengthen the cohesion of his foundation, John Baptist brought the Directors of the schools together in Rheims. He suggested that they make a retreat, 'a suggestion which was warmly welcomed'.[7] It started on the vigil of the Ascension and was to finish on Pentecost Sunday. In fact it went on until Trinity Sunday, 9 June.

Blain avers, 'We cannot mention … all the topics discussed during this assembly',[8] but he insists on pointing out, 'M. De La Salle did not try to lead them in one direction or another, nor to suggest to them his own views, nor insinuate his own ideas. He left them free to think and say whatever they liked'.[9]

As well as measures concerning the habit, regulations and food, by far the most important question focused on their eventual consecration to God.

'The Brothers wished to pronounce the three vows of poverty, chastity and obedience perpetually, but De La Salle did not wish to be precipitous. He advised them for the present to take the vow of obedience alone, and that for one year only, putting off for another time the fulfilment of their good intentions after they would have more time to reflect and test themselves'.[10] 'All acknowledged that he was right.'[11] 'He began the ceremony with the Mass of the Holy Spirit at which the Brothers received communion. He was the first to pronounce the vow of obedience, holding a candle in his hand, and the Brothers, approaching one after the other, took the same vow.'[12] 'This vow they continued to renew every year on the feast of Trinity Sunday'.[13]

The same evening they set out on pilgrimage to Our Lady of Liesse, near Laon. After walking for eight hours throughout the night they arrived at dawn on 10 June. John Baptist celebrated Mass, then each one returned to his community. In a chapel of that sanctuary a stained-glass window and a tablet commemorate the event.

In the course of that first assembly news came that Father Barré had died in Paris on 31 May.

A pre-novitiate

During the summer of 1686

> a young man, fifteen years of age applied for admission to the Institute. He was sent to the servant of God who, at the time, was still in Rheims and he admitted him although it was not customary to receive one so young. And some time after, three more applied for the same purpose. Then the servant of God, recognising in the induction of these young men that God was offering this opportunity for the good of his Institute, determined to form a little community of the four of them and of those who subsequently might apply. And so within two months God so blessed his initiative that this little community was made up of twelve young men for whom he drew up a set of regulations and put one of the older Brothers in charge of them. He himself often instructed them, being with them like one of themselves to win them all for Christ, following the example of the Apostle. This small community was completely separated from the Brothers. They were housed, not within, but next door to the Brothers' house and there was only one connecting gate to take them what they needed. And God so blessed the care taken of these young men that several reached a high degree of virtue. And it was a matter of great edification to see them in church and in the streets as modest as fervent religious. Almost weekly they received communion from the hand of the saintly priest and they were taught to make meditation.

Finally, they performed almost the same exercises as the novices now make at Saint Yon. From time to time the older and more fervent were given the Brothers' habit. Thus this community took the place of the novitiate.[14]

Some disciples

In August 1686, John Baptist made his way to the 'Desert', the Carmelite convent at La Garde Châtel, thirty kilometres south of Rouen, to make a private retreat. While there he received an urgent letter from Laon telling him that the two Brothers were sick and that one of them, Nicolas Bourlette, in the grip of a violent and unrelenting fever, was in danger of death. After a three day journey John Baptist arrived on the spot and found that Nicolas had been dead since 6 September. This Brother, a native of Rheims, had spent only three years in the Institute.

On 1 May 1687, Brother Jean Morice, just turned 17, died in Rheims.

In July of the same year a messenger brought the news that the Brother Director of Guise had fallen seriously ill. John Baptist left rue Neuve, on foot, early in the afternoon. It was very hot. His nose bled several times. At nightfall he rested for a while and spent several hours in prayer. He set out again at 3.00 am, celebrated Mass in Laon for the community, then reached Guise on a horse which had been lent him. Upon his arrival he embraced the Brother Director who was cured instantly and resumed his teaching a few days later. The miracle was well attested.[15]

In February 1688 the Mother House comprised twenty-five student teachers, twelve postulants and twelve novices. John Baptist was no longer living there as, from 24 February, he had settled in Paris with two Brothers.

2. The group takes on an identity

The circumstances

Whenever John Baptist had occasion to go to Paris—to meet his bishop, consult Father Barré, or visit his brothers—Jacques-Joseph who had become a Canon Regular of Sainte Geneviève in 1676, or Jean-Louis who had entered the Seminary of Saint Sulpice on 8 November 1682—he used to stay in Saint Sulpice, to which he remained very attached. Back in 1683 the parish priest had asked him to take charge of the school and the workshop in rue Princesse and John Baptist had promised him some Brothers.

The opportunity to fulfil his promise occurred when Archbishop Le

Tellier, wanting to keep him permanently in Rheims, 'offered to support the schools provided no new ones would be opened'.[16] This would have been, if not the death of the Institute, at least a restricting of it within the limits of one diocese. John Baptist pointed out the commitment he had given to the parish priest of Saint Sulpice, and hastened to reach Paris.

Soon after settling in, he signed an agreement with the parish priest, Father Claude Bottu de la Barmondière, his former professor in the seminary. This contract recognized the authority of the parish priest over the school and that of John Baptist de La Salle over the community.

Ten months later, however, on 7th January 1689, the parish priest resigned. He was replaced by one of his curates, Henri Baudrand de la Combe, whom John Baptist had chosen upon his arrival as his spiritual director. This new parish priest wanted the Brothers to wear ecclesiastical garb in school. With him in mind John Baptist wrote a *Memoir* preserved to this day in the archives of the Mother House.

The Memoir on the Habit [17]

Saint John Baptist de La Salle set out to defend the Brothers' habit from its eventual replacement by ecclesiastical dress. As was his wont, he proceeded extremely logically. Firstly he set out precisely the constitutive elements of his Community. Then he showed how these determined the design of the habit, the originality of the first justifying the 'singularity' of the second. This was done so well that the main interest in the text for readers today lies in the analysis the Founder makes of his work, an analysis which projects a clear light on his basic intentions.

Let us examine this identity card which he has drawn up for us.

The Community

What was its name? 'The Community of the Christian Schools'.[18] Let us recall that the word 'community' was ordinarily applied to the whole Institute which at that time enjoyed only a *de facto* existence with its tiny number of twenty or so Brothers, its Mother House in Rheims and a few other places of residence in some nearby towns. But it also happens, though very rarely, that Saint John Baptist de La Salle used 'community' to designate the group of Brothers living in a particular house.

What was its status? 'It is founded on Providence alone'.[19] This plainly meant that the schools had no fixed revenue on which they could depend.

Certain ones belonged to the Institute but others did not. The payment of the teachers' stipends remained at the discretion of the benefactors and would in the course of time be exposed to many vicissitudes. This precarious situation seems to have been borne serenely by the Brothers and did not present any obstacle to recruitment. 'This distinctive habit removes the doubts in the minds of those entering as to whether the community is stable and funded or not.'[20] John Baptist attributed this happy outcome to the wearing of the habit which, set in the framework of the Brothers' life, could, on the evidence, produce a feeling of solidity and unity. But, more deeply, must we not think that by renouncing his canonry and distributing his wealth to the poor, he would have been reaping the reward of his sacrifice and once and for all have eradicated the fears which disturbed the first teachers in 1682?

What was its objective? It was 'to conduct gratuitous schools in cities and towns only and teach catechism daily even on Sundays and feasts'.[21] The Rule of 1705 would present a fuller formulation. 'The end of this Institute is to give a Christian education to children and it is for this purpose that the Brothers keep schools, that, having the children under their care from morning until evening, they may teach them to lead good lives, by instructing them in the mysteries of our holy religion and by inspiring them with Christian maxims, and thus give them a suitable education.'[22] The *Memoir* keeps to the more immediate and more obvious obligations.

The members

Who were the members? They were laymen. 'Those who compose this community are all laymen.'[23]. And as De La Salle was writing only in opposition to adopting ecclesiastical garb, he insisted strongly on what distinguished priests from Brothers: 'laymen who have not studied [And this refers to study of the classics—Editor] and never will [in view of the priesthood] and who likewise exercise no church function nor wear the surplice in church'.[24] He even goes so far as to claim divine intervention, 'Providence has directed several to us who either have the tonsure or were advanced in their studies, but these have not remained'.[25] Blain offers a somewhat different version, 'Some of them were university students who gave up their studies and came to join him in spite of their parents' objections and of the frantic appeals of worldly people who did all they could to turn them away from him'.[26] The two versions are not incompatible.

Whatever the case may be, John Baptist de La Salle explained and justified the rejection of the priesthood for his Brothers. 'Those advanced in their studies are not refused but they are received on condition that they discontinue them because:

1. Study is not necessary for them.
2. It would be for them an occasion for quitting their state.
3. The obligations of community life and their school duties demand their entire time and energy.'[27]

This last phrase is crucial. It expresses very clearly what John Baptist de La Salle saw and wished the Brother to be. It is utterly regrettable that truncated quotations of it have been made, reducing it only to its second part and which by amputating the Founder's thought have distorted it.

It was neither exact nor Lasallian to write, as Yves Poutet did in 1992, 'the occupation of primary teaching requires a man's complete attention',[28] and again 'the job of Christian teaching in an elementary school requires a man's complete attention'.[29] If one takes into account only the profession and disregards any community obligation, it is inevitable that the Brother will be confused with the Christian teacher and what is meant for the first will be applied to the second. In the *Memoir on the Habit*, De La Salle, in portraying the Brother, takes as much precaution to distinguish him from the priest as from the country school master who divides his time and activity between the school and the church, in accordance with the formation received in the Seminary in rue Neuve and which is described in the *Memoir* in paragraphs 4, 5 and 6. This argumentation is more telling as nothing is found in these three paragraphs to preclude marriage.

The Brother is only a Brother to the extent that he interiorly integrates into his life 'the exercises of the community and … school duties'.[30] It is to the painting of this ideal that Saint John Baptist de La Salle devoted the *Memoir on the Habit*, in contrast to the *Meditations for the time of Retreat* which, being intended 'for the use of all persons working in the education of young people', make no allusion to the Community. This is so even though the word 'Brother' appears in the titles of meditations 202, 203, 206 and 208, and though we find in the second point of 208, 'Oh! what joy a Brother of the Christian Schools will have when he sees a great number of his students in possession of eternal happiness, for which they are indebted to him by the grace of Jesus Christ.' The Founder can easily be excused for letting slip a privileged thought for his sons in this sentence which, without any possible contradiction, can be applied like the rest of the text to all Christian teachers, whether Brothers or not.

Lifestyle

> Therein is led a life according to rule and in complete dependence on Providence, the members being completely poor.[31]

In the 17th century, the concept of a Rule was not the monopoly of religious. Christians serious about their faith placed themselves under the guidance of a spiritual director and tried to observe the regulations imposed on them. Such was the first attempt of John Baptist de La Salle to socialize the teachers whom Adrien Nyel had left to their 'whims'. 'He was in no hurry to give regulations to the Brothers … He preferred to have the rules practised for a long time before promulgating them definitively.'[32] As the Community grew and became aware of more sophisticated concerns, he took care to introduce new rules, 'more measured and better thought out than the previous ones'.[33] The result was that the Rule would no longer make do with regulating the behaviour of the group by means of a simple timetable; it would aim more at nourishing the spiritual life of each member, shaping his relationship with God and neighbour by the practice of the corresponding virtues. Thus, John Baptist could write on 18 April 1708 to Brother Hubert, Director of Guise, 'It is fidelity to the Rule which draws the blessing of God on a community'. [34]

The Brothers had numerous opportunities for practising obedience since 'dependence in everything' governed all their actions, in school as well as in community, where it 'established order, union, peace and tranquillity among those who belong to it'.[35] John Baptist sought to have them share in the great esteem he had for obedience. 'This virtue, more than any other, can be associated with the theological virtues, for faith is its principle and guide, it is always accompanied by hope and confidence in God, and it is a result of charity and the pure love of God.'[36] 'Let us, so to speak, make ourselves captives for the love of God through exact obedience and by a great fidelity to our Rules. This voluntary and loving obedience will make us truly free with the noble and glorious liberty of God's children.'[37] 'It is enough for an action to be performed through obedience for it to please God, when it is accomplished with such simplicity that you have in view only to obey.'[38]

The third aspect of community life that Saint John Baptist de La Salle drew attention to in the *Memoir on the Habit* goes beyond poverty, real though it was in the Lasallian houses. This was the will to be stripped of everything connected with material goods. The Brother liked to think of himself and to look upon himself as possessing nothing. Apart from his robe, mantle, hat and shoes he had no personal linen. Things he needed were simply put at his disposal by the Community. When he left a Community, he had to leave them there, without any certainty that he would find similar ones in the new house to which he was sent. Those customs would remain in the Institute until recent times. 'Let us not be surprised, then, when we lack something, even necessities, since at his birth Jesus was lacking everything. This is how we must be born in the spiritual life, dispossessed and deprived of everything'.[39]

Regularity, obedience, dire poverty, even if certain of their consequences had repercussions on the community stemmed above all from the personal asceticism of each Brother. That is why De La Salle hastened to supplement them with a virtue essentially of the social order, 'complete uniformity'. Each one was to practise behaviour in every way identical with that of his confreres and which, on occasion, could serve as a model. 'Since you live with your Brothers under the same rules and the same uniform behaviour, they observe you constantly, and so, it is especially to them that you should be an example in all things … You should keep all your rules exactly, not only to take the means given you by God for your own salvation, but also to edify your Brothers.'[40] 'Learn not to want to be distinguished from others, not to ask for or to seek any exemption in the practice of your rules'.[41] And the primary reason given to justify the adoption of the same garment for the Brothers would be, 'In every community in which the subjects possess nothing and have everything in common and do everything uniformly as in the Society of the Christian Schools, the habit is distinctive',[42] that is, particular and characteristic.

The *Memoir* implicitly evokes another aspect of the Brothers' lives, separation from the world. It seemed important in the eyes of the Founder that his sons have the feeling (he actually uses the word 'impression') 'that they belong to a community',[43] standing apart from 'the world' to guard themselves better from it. But it was also important that non-members, 'seculars', share this view. 'This special habit prompts seculars to look upon the members of this society as persons separated and retired from the world; and it appears very beneficial that this idea be entertained so that they would not frequent the world so easily, and be reserved towards seculars.'[44]

Rather than separation from the world, it would be better to speak of renunciation of the world, so much does De La Salle employ absolute terms to speak about it: 'You who have left the world, have you renounced it with as much enthusiasm as Saint Alexius? Was it your intention then, and is it still at present, never to have any more dealings with the world and to live in it totally unknown? If so, you will be in a position to labour usefully in your work.'[45] 'When you are obliged to leave your place of seclusion to be active in the world, you, too, should behave in such a manner that nobody will know who you are and that the very ones whom you teach will not know your name … You will not make people talk about you: you will be mere passers-by, solely concerned with doing God's work and causing Jesus to live in the souls of those who do not recognize him.'[46] 'You should consider yourself dead to the world, and you should have no dealings with it.'[47] For the feast of the Assumption he pushes the idea to its ultimate limits, 'Since we have left the world, nothing should be able to attach us to it. We should always be ready to die. This is the consequence of detachment from all things. We find it hard to die because we find it hard to leave what we love and what holds on to us'.[48]

Some have found these prescriptions unsuitable as addressed to men who, several times a day, had to cross the town to teach school or to take their pupils to church. On the other hand, others have judged them as so much more relevant. John Baptist de La Salle demonstrates a spiritual balance at the very heart of this tension, justifying it by the apostolic purpose of the Community. 'The work you do during the day does not prevent you from living in seclusion; love this seclusion and willingly preserve it … It will help you very much to acquire the perfection of your state and procure piety for your disciples.'[49] 'You should love seclusion where you can labour effectively at your own perfection, but you should leave it when God asks you to work for the salvation of the souls he has entrusted to you. As soon as God no longer calls you there, when the time of your work is over, you should … return to your solitude.'[50] 'You need to live in seclusion in order to learn the knowledge of salvation which you have to teach others. This is the benefit that you should receive from that kind of life.'[51]

On this precise point we can see a very concrete application of what we could call the unity of the Brother's life which the Founder condensed into the last sentence in the first section of the *Memoir on the Habit*, a sentence to which we must always come back to uphold the Lasallian charism: 'the obligations of community life and their school duties demand their entire time and energy'.[52]

'The whole man' desired by John Baptist de La Salle is the man preoccupied exclusively with the ministry of Christian education, apart from any other interest, a man who is undoubtedly not torn between other activities or varied concerns, one who, especially, has not a divided heart. Whether a Brother is in class or in the chapel, he is not doing anything other than working for the salvation of his students.

In *The Gospel Journey of St John Baptist de La Salle*, Brother Miguel Campos makes the following remark, 'The Community exercises are aimed at developing the evangelical dimension of the work of the Community; the work of the Community makes this evangelical life real in carrying out the mission of the Son of Man'.[53] If apostolic commitment is the mainspring of the life of the Brother, it is also its key if it gives rise to its constituent elements; it explains still better their synthesis.

Character of this community

The life of the Brother presented in the *Memoir on the Habit*, appears very exacting, very rigorous. It is truly a religious life. That is especially paradoxical since the Brother is a layman, but not a 'secular', and while not being a 'secular' he is in no way a religious! Canonists could very legitimately apply to the Lasallian Community the description the Founder gave of the Cenobites in the second point of his seventh meditation: 'a monstrosity'. (De La Salle uses this term because they attempted to live in a community without practising obedience—Editor.)

It is true that the expression 'religious community' occurs—once—in the text of the *Memoir on the Habit*, but it is not used of the Community of the Brothers. John Baptist de La Salle used it in quite a general manner. Besides, his reference is in the plural: 'A change in the habit appears to be a matter of some importance in a community, hence great precaution has been taken in most religious communities to avoid all occasions which might lead to such a change'. In the same article the expression 'regular religious' is found. But as it refers to religious communities of priests there was no temptation to say that the Brothers were regulars!

If the Brothers had been religious in 1690, the *Memoir on the Habit* would have provided the Founder with a wholly natural opportunity to proclaim it. But if the Brothers in 1690 had been religious, he would not have needed to have recourse to all his argumentation to save their dress. It would have sufficed to shelter behind the customs of the congregation.

His great difficulty was that at the period when he wrote his *Memoir*, the Brothers were not religious despite the life they were leading. If they passed for such in the eyes of good Christian people ('this special habit prompts seculars to look upon the members of this society as persons separated and retired from the world'[54]) they did not pull the wool over the eyes of the learned or of bishops who stood by the adage of the Council of Trent, as quoted in part in the first point of Meditation 60, 'The habit does not make the religious: it is consecration which does so'. No more than seven or eight members of the 1686 Assembly had pronounced only private vows.

Here let us cite an interesting remark of Brother Henri Bédel in his *Origines*: 'However even more than these traits, which may be called exterior ones, what characterized the Brothers' Community was the fervour of its members'.[55] Blain, in particular, reports evidence of it in recalling the memory of Brothers who died young in the course of the years, Brother Jean-François in 1684, Brother Nicolas Bourlette in 1686 and Jean Morice on 1 May 1687.[56]

In a meditation entitled 'On the manner in which we should love God,' Saint John Baptist de La Salle would later write,

> It is truly to sacrifice your life for God, to spend it only for him. This is what you can do in your profession and your work, not being concerned if you die in a few years, provided you save yourself and win souls for God. They will help you to rise to heaven because you have tried to help them to procure admittance there, have taught them how to enter, and have helped them to take all possible means of doing so. In this way you will show God that you love him with all your soul.[57]

It was this fervour which would attract to Saint John Baptist de La Salle new candidates. Among these were children who were no older than he was when he himself received the tonsure.

Lasallian Texts

Philosophy of Regulations

The citations which follow show how De La Salle's underlying philosophy about the need for consistency on following principles pervades his writings [Editor].

Man is so subject to slackening and even to changing that he needs written rules to keep him within the bounds of his duties and prevent him from introducing novelty or destroying what has been wisely established (*Conduct of Schools*, Preface, p. 45).

There are few changes which are not prejudicial to a community, especially in things which might appear of little consequence.

Changes are always a mark of inconstancy and give evidence of but little stability; nevertheless stability in the practices and points of rule appear one of the chief supports of a community.

One change in a community is a wedge for others and ordinarily leaves a bad impression on all in the community or at least on some of them.

Most of the disorders and irregularities in communities come from a marked tendency to introduce changes. That is why it is an accepted maxim by those experienced in community life that before introducing anything new in a community it is necessary to reflect maturely and examine the good and bad consequences it may have. And after having once established a thing it would require an urgent and imperious necessity to supplant it.[58]

Author's note: The first text from the *Conduct of Schools* is about 'the individual', the rest are about 'community'. Here the word 'community' means religious institute.

The personal regulations John Baptist de La Salle imposed on himself

In whatever situation I may find myself, I will always follow a daily schedule and regulations with the grace of God, in which alone I place my trust to carry this out, for this is something I have never been able to accomplish by myself (Rule 10 of 'Rules I have imposed upon myself', translated by Edwin Bannon FSC).

Young as De La Salle was, he always liked to live by rule; regularity, a cherished virtue, governed all his conduct. He had seen this attitude exemplified at the Seminary of Saint Sulpice and from the first had profited by this manner of acting. In that abode of virtue he had experienced for himself and witnessed in the lives of others what purity of conduct, what innocence of life, what solidity of virtue such fidelity to a rule leads to, especially a rule that is prudent and well tailored to human weakness. Regularity, he knew, must be universal, exact, and inspired by inner conviction. He made it a strict duty for himself, both inside and outside the seminary, to be perfectly regular. He liked everything to be done at its proper time (Blain, vol.1, bk.1, p. 41).

He could not bring himself to let the schoolmasters continue to live as they pleased, with no order or standards of behaviour, and consequently without true piety. He would have preferred to stop looking after them entirely. Himself a man who lived by rule, he wanted this same attitude to prevail wherever he went. As he could not live without order, he could not permit those under his care to live without a determined schedule (Blain, vol.1, bk.1, p. 82).

At first De La Salle did not bring the masters to live in his house. He limited himself to inviting them to come for meals so that he could begin to regulate their actions. After morning mental prayer they heard Mass at six o'clock, then came to his house which was close by theirs. They remained with him until time for night prayers after which they went back home to sleep. In the canon's house there already existed a fixed regulation. Good books were read during meals, and prayers were recited at fixed times. Thus the presence of the schoolmasters did not call for any great changes in the daily routine. At this time, however, the meals were served in the dining room with individual portions for each (Blain, vol.1, bk.1, p. 86)

He transformed his house into a kind of hostel to which country priests often came. (Blain, vol.1 bk.1, p. 53; Bernard, *CL*, 4, 25). A set of simple regulations made common life bearable ... Rather than strict regulations insensitively imposed ... there was an openness to the others which, little by little, brought about modifications in the organisation of family life (Y. Poutet, *St Jean-Baptiste de la Salle*, p. 24).

The road to sanctity in his Institute would not be submission to regulations as in the Seminary, but the interior life through faith which confers eternal value on the slightest details of existence (Y. Poutet, pp. 236-237).

Unity in the Brother's life
(according to Sunday Meditation No 64, 2)

'God has put you in charge of instructing children...'

three terms	God	(a) the author
	you	(b) the agent
	the children	(c) the beneficiaries
two actions	(a) duty	(b) mission
	(b) to instruct	(c) the ministry

'You make yourself expert in the art of speaking to God, of speaking about God, and of speaking for God ...'

a single ministerial art
expressed in three ways: (1) speaking to
                               (2) speaking about
                               (3) speaking for

'Be convinced that you (b) will never speak well to your students (c) and win (3) them over to God (a) except in so far as you have learned well how to speak to (1) him and to speak about (2) him.

the purpose: conversion and salvation (3)
the means: prayer (1) and instruction (2)

We, *for our part, will devote ourselves to prayer and to serving the word.* (Acts 6:4)

Community and unity of life of the Brother

The obligations of community life and their school duties demand their entire time and energy (Fitzpatrick, *Memoir on the habit*, p. 191).

Do you exercise your zeal for your neighbour in such a way that all you do to help others sanctify themselves does not prevent you in any way from being exact and assiduous in all the exercises of your community? Are you convinced that God will bless your labours for your neighbour only to the degree that you are faithful to your rules, because you will not obtain any graces to contribute to the salvation of others except insofar as you yourself are faithful to grace and have the true spirit of your vocation? (*Meditations*, 128, 3)

Are you completely faithful to the Rule in your community? This is the sure way to draw down on yourselves the graces of God you need to fulfil the duties of your state and the ministry to which God has called you. The more exact you are in the observance of the Rule, the more you will be able to lead children to God and to procure for them a true and solid piety. Since this is the purpose of your state, take the means that are most appropriate for you, and which God requires of you in order to succeed (*Meditations*, 131, 2).

To make your zeal useful to others, you should first exercise it in regard to yourselves and your community. With this in mind, and in regard to yourselves, you must watch over yourselves without pardoning the slightest fault, or let anything escape you which can in the least displease God without procuring for yourselves a penance able to remedy the evil. You should also, out of zeal for discipline, contribute so well to establish observance of the Rule in your community that it may become a heaven on earth where charity and peace reign (*Meditations*, 83, 1).

Community, sanctity, happiness

It is by withdrawing yourself from the world that you consecrated yourself to God to live in this community with a complete detachment from everything in the world which is able to satisfy your senses. In order to settle down here in this community, you should consider the day you made this move as the one on which your happiness on earth began. But it was not for that day alone that you should have consecrated yourself to God, since you made a consecration of your soul on that occasion, and since your soul will live forever, your dedication to God must be forever. If you have begun this on earth, it should have only been to carry out here a sort of apprenticeship of what you will do eternally in heaven (*Meditations*, 191, 1).

… I express to you my very humble gratitude … [that] it is you who have withdrawn me from all the situations in which I could still commit more sins, by withdrawing me from the world by placing me in community (*Encountering God in the Depths of the Mind and Heart*, 1995, no. 149 a & b, p. 179).

I must consider the advantage I have of being in community as my supreme happiness on earth (*Encountering God in the Depths of the Mind and Heart*, no. 149 c, p. 180).

Because in your state you are called to procure the sanctification of your pupils, you should be holy yourself in no ordinary degree, for you must communicate this holiness to them both by your good example and by the words of salvation which you must address to them every day. Interior application to prayer, love for your exercises, fidelity in performing them well and in carrying out all the other community practices will especially help you to acquire this holiness and the perfection that God wishes you to have (*Meditations*, 39, 2).

Since God has given you the grace of calling you to live in community, there is nothing that you should more earnestly ask of him than this union of mind and heart with your Brothers. Only by means of this union will you acquire that peace which ought to be all the joy of your life (*Meditations*, 39, 3).

This place is the gate of heaven, because it enables us to take the path leading to heaven and prepares us to enter it. This is the first purpose you should have had when you entered this community and what ought to keep you here. It is for this end that we live withdrawn from the world and why we commit ourselves to all kinds of exercises of piety (*Meditations* 77, 1).

Chapter 5

To live on
bread alone

1. The vow of 1691

The Communities of rue Neuve

The communities at Rheims did not easily accept their Founder's departure. Of the 16 brothers that made up the community in 1688, eight left in the course of that same year, repulsed by the harsh way of acting by the Director whom John Baptist had appointed to take his place. Once the teacher-trainees had completed their formation, they returned to the parishes they came from, thereby closing at the same time the Seminary for country schoolmasters.

Faced with this situation, John Baptist De La Salle, after a meeting with all the Brothers in Rheims, decided it was preferable that the youngest should go to Paris where they would be under the care of Brother Henri Lheureux. 'He was the first to join the Institute of the Christian Schools. De La Salle had seen in him an uncommon virtue, great discernment of mind, affable manners and a talent for speaking.'[1] He was one of those who, after the assembly of 1686, made the vow of obedience. Then the following year when John Baptist asked the Brothers to elect one of their number as Superior, he was the one for whom the majority of votes were cast. But the Vicars-General of Rheims 'were quite offended that a priest, doctor, and former canon of the cathedral should be thus obedient to a simple layman'.[2] John Baptist, forced to resume his duties as Superior which he had wished to relinquish, subsequently planned to arrange that 'he whom he would have picked for his successor'[3] should proceed to the priesthood. He had him study Latin, and from October 1687 begin his theological studies with the Canons Regular of the Abbey of St Denis in Rheims. When he summoned Brother Henri to Paris, he wanted him, while looking after postulants, to continue his studies at the Sorbonne University until he was ready for ordination.

The school in the rue du Bac

The school in the rue Princesse, once it had been re-organized by De La Salle, was very well administered and managed by its two Brothers. It prospered so well that the parish priest of St Sulpice thought it would be good for a second school to be opened on a corner site where the rue du Bac met the rue de Lille. John Baptist arranged for two more Brothers, Nicolas Vuyart and Bernard Legentil, to come from Rheims to begin teaching in January 1690.

The schoolmasters of the 'little schools', worried by the competition arising from the fact that the new schools were conducted free of charge while their own pupils were required to pay a fee, were quick to react. Four of these teachers wearing their gowns invaded the premises of the two classrooms, made off with the desks, seats and books and then lodged a complaint with the principal Precentor,[4] a certain Claude Joly.

Joly, on 23 February, gave judgment against the school even though he had not issued any decree for its closure. John Baptist was no lover of litigation but the parish priest Father Baudrand, proprietor of the school and its furnishings, required De La Salle to lodge an appeal with the Parliament. The judgment, brought down on 18 March, was favorable to De La Salle. The masters of the 'little schools' made a counter appeal. The new judgment was likewise in favor of the Brothers. The masters were obliged to return the furnishings 'to M. De La Salle and his associates on the condition these latter continue to teach out of charity the children in their schools and to receive no recompense therefrom'.[5] Had they ever done anything other than that?

Sickness and death

At the beginning of November, John Baptist de La Salle, despite feeling physically weak, travelled on foot to Rheims where two months earlier he had appointed as Director Brother Jean Henry, who was only 19 years old. On arrival De La Salle fell ill. His grandmother, Perrette Lespagnol, came to visit him. He met her in the parlour 'in order not to transgress the rules of the House'.[6]

In December, one of the Brothers at Rue Princesse departed from the community. To take his place in class as best he could John Baptist returned to Paris. At Christmas he returned to rue Neuve leaving Brother Henri Lheureux in charge of rue Princesse. 'No sooner had the latter [De La Salle] reached Rheims than a letter arrived informing him that Brother Henri had fallen ill. Another told him the case was serious; a third declared the doctors had given up hope.'[7] He set out at once for Paris and made as much haste as possible. But Brother Henri had been buried for two days when De La Salle reached Paris around midnight. The first onslaught of sorrow made him shed tears, but afterwards he declared that the sudden demise of Brother Henri was a warning from Heaven, indicating that the Institute should not include priests among its members'.[8]

The year 1691 then, began with a bereavement, the third for the Paris Community since Brother Louis had died in 1688 and Brother Nicolas the year following.

As far as John Baptist was concerned, 'his illness returned just as the doctors had predicted. He was compelled to take to his bed where he stayed for six weeks. He felt so ill that he thought he was going to die.'[9] Helvetius, the Court Doctor, who because of his esteem for John Baptist de La Salle, cared for the Brothers' health without requiring fees, suggested a treatment be given which could just as easily kill as cure the patient.[10] John Baptist received viaticum from Father Baudrand 'who came in procession with his clergy to administer it … after the ceremony was completed, he took the prescribed remedy which had the hoped-for salutary effect.'[11]

The Heroic Vow

A long convalescence was imperative for John Baptist. He used the situation to make a long retreat. His Institute was undergoing something similar to what he had lived through: a sickness which could lead to death. A remedy had to be found. He resolved 'to establish somewhere near Paris a house where convalescent Brothers could go to recover their health: to gather all the Brothers there during the vacation and to have them make a retreat in order to help recover, along with their first fervour, the spirit and grace of their state; to establish a novitiate for the training of candidates'.[12] He confirmed his decision to forbid the Brothers to study for the priesthood, and decided also that they would henceforth take a religious name. He arranged also for regular monthly correspondence with each of them.

These means, the fruit of ordinary common sense, seemed to the Founder to be insufficient because they were purely human. Drawing on his faith he planned a further means which was wholly spiritual, namely 'to associate with himself two Brothers whom he considered the most apt to sustain the fledgling community and to bind the three of them by an irrevocable bond to pursue the establishment of the Institute'.[13]

No one would have been better suited to this plan than Brother Henri Lheureux but God had arranged otherwise for him. De La Salle's choice had then been directed to two of his longest serving companions, Nicolas Vuyart, who had been with him since 1682, and Gabriel Drolin, who, at age 20 had abandoned his studies for the priesthood in order to join the Community.[14]

At Vaugirard, De La Salle rented a dwelling which had a vegetable garden. There he summoned all the Brothers for a retreat commencing on 8 September and lasting a full month. After the retreat the older Brothers returned to their schools while the youngest who had been in the Community for only two or three years remained behind. Eight in number, these latter made a kind of novitiate until Christmas. Every week the Brothers living in Paris came back to relax from their work and especially to renew their fervour. On 21 November, De La Salle arrived with Nicolas Vuyart and Gabriel Drolin and with the utmost secrecy pronounced the following vow:

> Most Holy Trinity, Father, Son and Holy Spirit, prostrate with the utmost profound respect before Thy infinite and adorable majesty, we consecrate ourselves entirely to Thee to procure with all our ability and efforts the establishment of the Society of the Christian Schools, in the manner which will seem to us most agreeable to Thee and most advantageous to the said Society. And for this purpose, I, John Baptist de La Salle , priest: I, Nicolas Vuyart, and I, Gabriel Drolin, from now on and forever until the last surviving one of us, or until the complete establishment of the said Society make the vow of association and union to bring about and maintain the said establishment, without being able to withdraw from this obligation, even if only we three remained in the said Society, and if we were obliged to beg for alms and to live on bread alone. In view of which we promise to do, all together and by common accord, everything we shall think in conscience and regardless of any human consideration, to be for the greater good of the said Society.

Done on the 21st of November, feast of the Presentation of Our Lady, 1691. In testimony of which we have signed ... [15]

Thus there were three Brothers in the presence of the Most Holy Trinity. ' For where two or three meet in my name, I shall be there with them'. (Matthew 18:20.) The three Divine Persons are named, Father, Son and Holy Spirit, as well as the three making the vow, John Baptist de La Salle, Nicolas Vuyart and Gabriel Drolin. And just as they are united in the name of the Trinity which begins the formula, so the three 'I's' are caught up again in the 'we's' which follow immediately and already embody the association before it becomes the object of a vow. Before they even pronounce their engagement, the three men have been united in their intention to associate and the final statement, 'In testimony of which we have signed', ratifies and gives evidence of its fulfilment. Between these two 'we's', a new marker has been raised for the Institute, a new foundation stone laid for its construction.

The aim of this dialogue between God and the Lasallian trio was itself clearly set out, as being 'the establishment of the Society of the Christian Schools'. It was not a question of anything else, either of children or of the poor. Even if these were now more than ever present in the thinking of the three signatories to the vow formula, the text itself makes absolutely no mention of them. The schools even do not rate a mention except as part of the title which John Baptist gave, in the *Memoir on the Habit*, to the 'Community of the Christian Schools',[16] which in the vow formula he describes as the 'Society of the Christian Schools'.

Why this change of wording?

The word 'community' for John Baptist De La Salle has a totally religious meaning, which justifies its usage in the *Memoir on the Habit* and in all official texts. The Founder will use the word 'community', even up to the time of his death, twice as often as the word 'society' (202 examples as against 104). The latter term has a much wider significance, as it includes at one and the same time the school aspect of Lasallian activities as well as its religious character ('with what devotion the Rosary should be recited in the Society').[17] John Baptist defines a society 'as a gathering together in one and the same body'[18] including in this way in a very forceful fashion the notions of union, solidarity and sharing. That is why he ordinarily uses the word 'Society' to describe the Church. After a few years he replaced it with the word 'Institute'. 'The Institute of the Brothers of the Christian Schools is a Society in which profession is made of keeping schools gratuitously.'[19] Let us note that at the time of the Founder, numerous societies, mainly clerical came into existence, requiring according to canon law a minimum of three members.

We have already quoted elsewhere the prayer John Baptist addressed to God in 1683 when he was wondering as to whether or not he should use his wealth to found his schools:

> It is not up to me but to you to establish and maintain a community of teachers. You alone are aware of how to bring this about in the manner most pleasing to you. [20]

This spirit of trust in God was always with the Founder. But now that he has associated with himself two of his Brothers with a view to establishing the Institute, he nuances his prayer to say 'in the manner which will seem to us most agreeable to thee and most advantageous to the said Society.' In this way fidelity to God's will is aligned with a community discernment of the Holy Spirit:—'The ordinary way in which the Spirit is revealed is through a community working together to discover the needs of the world and of the Church'[21]—and it seemed to the three that the manner most advantageous to the Society and so most agreeable to God was exactly the profession both from a divine and human viewpoint of this Trinitarian vow. The terms describing the engagement are used with almost juridical precision: it is of the utmost importance to know and state clearly what is being promised. But what is more remarkable is the absolute nature of these terms reinforced by their repetition. For example:

> Entirely … unto the complete establishment … with all our ability and efforts … most agreeable … most advantageous … for the greater good … forever until the last … without being able to withdraw … regardless of any human consideration … all together by common accord …

All this indicates a style of writing and a vocabulary which we discover again in the Testament of John Baptist De La Salle. So he signs the text of the vow formula and proves, if need be, its origin: made out in the handwriting of the Founder, it is presented by him in person to his two companions who accept and make it their own.

Undeniably, the salient expression is 'even if we were obliged to beg for alms and live on bread alone'. This expression will be used again in the 1694 vow formula and will continue to be so used until a date that lies between 7 June 1705 and 25 September 1716.[22]

We cannot be more precise with this date because of the loss of the register of vows. The phrase is found in the *Collection* until 1886, in the chapter explaining 'what are the obligations arising from the vows of the Brothers of the Christian Schools ... if it should happen that everything is lacking in the Society, never to abandon one's state for this reason but rather to resolve to beg for alms and live on bread alone in order never to abandon the said Society nor the Schools'.[23] Indeed, John Baptist De La Salle alludes to this in his meditation for the feast of Saint Cajetan:

> You cannot carry disinterestedness too far in your work; it is the poor that you have to teach; instruct them by your example; in order to teach them to love poverty, let your disinterestedness lead you to practice it as far as it pleases God. You know, too, that you have committed yourself to keep schools gratuitously and to live on bread alone if need be, rather than accept anything. Be on your guard, therefore never to receive anything whatever, either from the students or from their parents.[24]

2. The Vows of 1694

Extreme Poverty

The expression 'to beg for alms and live on bread alone' coming from the pen of John Baptist De La Salle was never meant to be just idle words or a quirk of style. Following the distribution of his own wealth, he had already had the experience of begging as pointed out by Blain :

> Deprived of everything and having become poorer than those he had fed he in his turn sacrificing his self love, went from house to house, asking for alms. After several refusals he received from a good woman a loaf of black bread which out of respect he ate kneeling and with a joy impossible to describe.[25]

Similar situations arose for him and the Brothers, since the historians have indicated that, in his lifetime, there were about ten famines that could be described as great or very severe. All the Brothers, who, following his example, had pronounced the same vows using the same vow formula, were fully aware of the meagreness and fragility of the resources of an Institute which had no other support than that of Divine Providence. At least Providence never failed him.

Living conditions in the Vaugirard dwelling, situated in a country area

The young de La Salle with his grandmother.
Stained glass, Oakhill Chapel.

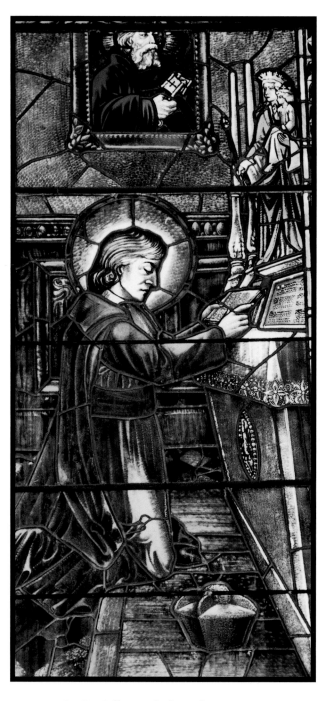

De La Salle spends the night in prayer.
Stained glass, Oakhill Chapel.

De La Salle, guide and teacher of his Brothers.
Stained glass, Oakhill Chapel.

De La Salle teaching at Grenoble.
Stained glass, Oakhill Chapel.

about three kilometres from St Sulpice were such as to suggest almost complete destitution. 'A few benches to sit on, a few straw pallets laid on the floor were all the furnishings available. Open to the elements, the house did not shelter its inhabitants either from the wind, the snow or the rain. Windows and doors were out of joint; windows were broken and the holes in the walls of the house [which had been unoccupied for some time] which nobody thought of repairing'[26] made it a real abode of penance. All this did not prevent John Baptist De La Salle from summoning the Brothers to make a retreat there in September 1692, and to open his first novitiate in October of that same year. Six novices took the habit on 1 November.

However, the winter of 1693, 'so disastrous on account of the famine and pestilence which desolated France',[27] was even worse in this place 'where fire was forbidden'.[28] While Louis XIV decreed (as he did only three times during his reign) that the relics of Saint Genevieve should be carried in procession, the Brothers lacked all material resources, 'on one occasion far from being discouraged when the community lacked even bread and had little hope of getting any … the Brother in charge of provisions looked everywhere for food … he could obtain only a small bit of black bread. De La Salle had this distributed among the Brothers without taking any himself; but they refused to touch it unless he took some also'.[29] Several times the Brother in charge of provisions was attacked and robbed. Some hungry poor came to the novitiate in hope of being fed, but they could not for very long put up with the austerities. The Founder himself was once attacked by robbers who seized his cloak, but seeing it was so old and worn, they returned it to him.

To safeguard the livelihood and security of the novices, it was necessary to bring them to rue Princesse. However, the parish priest of St Sulpice, who foresaw that parish resources for charity were diminishing refused to take any responsibility for them and used the situation as a pretext for withholding the five hundred livres he used to give to the community for the upkeep of the Brothers. Then 'about the middle of January, 1694, when the famine was raging most cruelly, whether Baudrand had exhausted all the funds he had left, or whether he felt he owed no special consideration to the Brothers over other needy persons, he informed John Baptist that he would not give him anything more and that he would consider what he had given him at the end of the previous year as an advance on the salaries of the Brothers who taught in the parish.'[30]

The first general chapter

Such an intolerable situation could not be anything but a source of joy to John Baptist De La Salle. Faithful to the advice of Nicolas Barré 'that those who work in schools should share the same fate as the Son of Man',[31] he used to say with pleasure, 'Our brothers will succeed only if they remain poor. They shall lose the spirit of their calling as soon as they become preoccupied with the commodities of life'.[32] So did De La Salle set about establishing his objectives. Having brought the novices back to Vaugirard in April 1694, he began a month's retreat, during which he wrote a Rule of fifteen chapters, this being the first written rule in the Institute. He sent a copy of the rule to twelve brothers who, from among the thirty that made up the Community, held special responsibilities. These he then summoned to Vaugirard for an assembly, which came to be recorded as the first General Chapter. Begun on 30 May the Feast of Pentecost, it finished its work on the following Sunday 6 June.

The Rules, which had already been practised for several years, and which during this period had been the object of many discussions, were finally unanimously approved. A second matter of importance dealt with the vows, which required considerable debate. A final decision led to the retention of those vows which had been professed in 1688 and 1691, namely those of association, stability and obedience.

The first profession of perpetual vows

On Sunday 6 June 1694, Feast of the Most Holy Trinity, 'he retired with these twelve Brothers into a remote room of the house, where they held the ceremony at their ease and in full liberty.'[33] Wearing his surplice and kneeling before the Most Blessed Sacrament exposed, and holding a lighted candle in his hand, he was the first to read his act of consecration. He was followed each in turn by his fellow associates. 'Fourteen copies of this formula have come down to us: thirteen in the *Booklet of the First Vows*, the fourteenth on a single sheet, written entirely in his own handwriting. This letter is one of the most precious relics left to us by John Baptist de La Salle'.[34] This is the text:

> Most Holy Trinity, Father, Son and Holy Ghost, prostrate with the most profound respect before your infinite and adorable Majesty, I consecrate myself entirely to you to procure your glory as far as I am able and as you will require of me. And for this reason, I, John Baptist de La Salle, priest,

promise and vow to unite myself and live in society with the Brothers to keep together and by association gratuitous schools, in whatever place, even should I be obliged to ask for alms and live on bread alone, or to do anything in the said society at which I shall be employed whether by the body of the society or by the superiors who shall have the government thereof. Wherefore I promise and vow obedience, whether to the body of the society or to its Superiors, which vows of association, as well as of stability in the said Society, and of obedience I promise to keep inviolably all my life time. In testimony whereof I have signed. Done at Vaugirard this sixth day of June, the Feast of the Most Holy Trinity in the year 1694. De La Salle [35]

The heroic vow of 1691 and the perpetual vows of 1694, both follow the same procedure and are expressed in much the same wording. Yet there are significant differences between the two. Just as the first vow formally makes a striking impression because of its unusual character—its limitation to three persons only, rendered null and void on the occasion of the death of 'the last surviving member' or 'at the complete establishment of the said Society', restricted above all in its aim which does not go beyond 'the said society'—so the second formula is presented as both official and necessary. How many brothers year by year, would be called upon to pronounce their vows as their turn came around? Whatever the differences between the two, we may ask if without the first there would have been the others to follow?

A very strict logic, nourished completely by faith, produced this vow formula. Addressed to the most Holy Trinity and taking as its objective a most elevated intention 'to procure your glory as far as I am able and as you will require of me', it proceeds to list the successive degrees of consecration:

1. I promise and vow to unite myself and remain in Society with the Brothers …

2. … to keep together and by association gratuitous schools …

3. Wherefore, I now promise and vow obedience and sealing all this for eternity: which vows of association and of stability in the said Society, and of obedience, I promise to keep inviolably during my lifetime.

The essential element of this text is found in 'association'. It is the pivotal point around which the whole document is structured. In the mind of the Founder, this theme of association determines both the manner of living in community ('to unite myself and live in society with the Brothers') and the way of carrying out the society's apostolate ('to keep together and by association gratuitous schools'). The schools appear in their own right, and it is for their advantage and no longer for the establishment of the Institute that the contract 'to ask for alms and live on bread alone' is seen as the last resort.

Finally, the two other vows seem like off-shoots of the first. In proportion as the association is vowed for life, stability in the Institute would seem to follow naturally. And obedience is the most immediate result to follow from association. This is formally expressed in the preceding word 'wherefore': now that I have made this solemn promise:

> I must now take the means to put it into practice in my daily living and I see no better way to do this than by obeying.

The rather complicated grammatical construction at the end of the sentence, by giving association a place apart, emphasizes its priority: 'which vows of association as well as stability in the said Society and of obedience' though it in no way relegates these last two vows to a position of secondary importance.

Included in the decisions made by John Baptist de La Salle, during his long convalescence of 1691, to improve the human and spiritual conditions of his followers was that of handing over to serving Brothers the material management of each house. This alleviated the lot of those who until then had carried out this function in addition to their schoolwork. The first of these serving Brothers began work as from the following year. Since the Founder, influenced by scruple as much as by exactitude in his thinking, did not wish to impose on these new Brothers an engagement that they would never have to fulfil (namely to teach class) he eliminated from their vow formula the expression 'to keep together and by association gratuitous schools'.

This alteration in the text indicated that he considered this phrase as the logical grammatical complement not to the past participle 'associated' which immediately precedes but with the verbal phrase 'to unite myself and live in society with the Brothers of the Christian Schools'.

In this way he expressed the purpose not so much of the association of the Brothers but rather of the contract made by the individual in their Society. Similarly the 'or' which follows 'sent' (*wherever I may be sent*) links 'to do in the said society' with 'to keep together and by association'. For the professed serving Brother this would mean being employed at work other than teaching (*to do anything in the Society at which I shall be employed*). This 'or' stands out clearly in the vow formula of the serving Brothers with no longer any reason for its being there.

In the present vow formula. presented in article 25 of the 1987 Rule, this same 'or' has been replaced by 'and' (1 promise to go wherever I may be sent and do whatever I may be assigned ...' Since then we can regard this coordinate conjunction (*or*) as linking the verbs 'to unite myself and live' with two different complements which are on the one hand 'wherever I may be sent' and on the other hand 'to do anything at which I shall be employed.'[36]

Over and above all these grammatical considerations, which are not just idle curiosities, it is undoubtedly more important to highlight the unity of structure which controls the first two paragraphs of the vow formula in current use. Taken together these two paragraphs cover in fact the same three stages

1. A formula of consecration:

I consecrate myself entirely to you to procure your glory.
I promise to unite myself and live in society with the Brothers of the Christian Schools who are associated to keep together and by association for the service of the poor.

2. A form of engagement which is radical:

... wherever I may be sent and to do whatever I may be assigned;

3. A referral to authority:

... as you will require of me whether by the Body of the Society or by its Superiors.

We must explain that the provisions of the second paragraph make precise and explicit the corresponding provisions of the first paragraph. It is the integration into the Institute which gives an incarnational reality to the consecration to God, just as to keep together and by association schools for the service of the poor establishes a way of procuring God's glory. It is likewise the availability (*disponibilité*) in regard to place and employment that allows us to gauge the breadth or extent of the possibilities of each individual that makes the act of consecration. Finally, the Brothers believe that the Body of the Institute or its Superiors are truly the ordinary medium whereby God makes known his request and will. The synthetic nature of the vow formula offers us an abundance of spiritual riches within its framework.

The act of election

On the day following the vow ceremony, 7 June 1694, John Baptist de La

Salle assembled the Brothers once again to inform them of his intention to resign as Superior, 'seeing that the good of the Institute demanded they choose one of their own whom they would judge most capable of taking over this charge'. [37] 'So when the votes were cast, and the ballots counted, every last one had voted to put back in the first place the one who had wished to relinquish it'.[38] Surprised and worried, he asked for a second vote, which only confirmed the first. 'Then the Brothers, feeling themselves emboldened by these repeated and precise indications of where the divine will lay, took the liberty of pointing out to him that he was bound to submit'.[39] He had to yield to their wishes, but he made them draw up an official declaration to be added to the thirteen formulas of perpetual vows, and this they all signed.

> We, the undersigned after associating ourselves with John Baptist de La Salle, priest, to keep together gratuitous schools, by the vows which we have pronounced yesterday, declare that as a consequence of these vows and of the association which we have formed by them, we have chosen as our Superior, John Baptist de La Salle, to whom we promise obedience and entire submission, as well as to those whom he will assign to us as our Superiors. We also declare that it is our understanding that the present election will not have the force of precedent for the future. Our intention is that after the said John Baptist de La Salle, and forever in the future, no one shall be received among us or chosen as Superior who is a priest or who has received Sacred Orders; and that we will not have or accept any Superior who has not associated himself with us, and has not made vows like us and like all those who will be associated with us in the future.
>
> Done at Vaugirard, on 7 June 1694.[40]

This act of election satisfied all parties, the Brothers who retained John Baptist de La Salle as their leader and the Founder himself who won the assurance that henceforth only a Brother would direct the Institute. As for the Institute itself, it had taken a giant step forward by this act. It found itself given a Superior who arose from among their ranks; it was given also a regular and responsible Assembly, constituting what the 1694 vow formula described as 'the Body of this Society'; it was given vows, which while consecrating each Brother to God, acted among them as a means of cohesion, more powerful than a name and a habit. The foundation in the capital, seen as a springboard for expansion throughout the whole of France, seemed to have a solid and successful base and was crowned by a novitiate which served both as an agent for forming new members and for strengthening the earlier members.

What was still lacking for the Institute was official recognition by the State and the Church. The first was given on 28 September 1724 by *Letters Patent* of Louis XV, the second on 26 January 1725 by the Bull of Approbation, *In apostolicae dignitatis solio*, which was registered with the Rouen Parliament on 12 May of the same year, or five and six years respectively after the death of John Baptist De La Salle. Nicolas Vuyart had also died by this time and only Brother Gabriel Drolin remained till 1733 as the 'last surviving member' of the heroic vow, to witness the 'fulfillment of his [and their] generous ambition to bring to a satisfactory conclusion the vow made thirty-four years earlier'.[41]

The canonical status of the Institute

The official recognition of the Institute was followed by the introduction of the vows of poverty and chastity which, together with that of obedience, took prior place before the vows of association and stability in the vow formula. This was a singular change, which in no way, however, changed the Institute's status. Brother Hermans, who declares that 'all the evidence suggests that the 1694 vows, which were simple and private, did not in any way involve the juridical consequences of the 'monastic profession',[42] also adds that the 'pontifical document [Bull of Approbation] does not turn the Institute into a religious order, nor does it declare the vows of the Brothers to be solemn vows: quite to the contrary the document allows the Society of the Christian Schools to retain its mark of an association with simple vows, without in any way aligning its members with Regulars'[43] (i.e., members of religious orders in the canonical sense).

The Institute was required to await the reform of the Code of Canon Law, which widened the criteria for the definition of religious life for congregations with simple vows to be admitted along with the traditional orders, to that status. There was a further wait, until 25 March 1996, for a pontifical document, *Vita consecrata,* to speak for the first time of 'religious brothers'.

It is far better, of course, to try to live out to the full one's vocation than to receive the official decree which confirms it. While waiting to be able to describe the Brothers as 'lay religious' let us say, for this period which concerns us here, that they are 'religious laymen' with emphasis on the word 'religious'.

Their three vows of association, stability and obedience did not confer on them some new form of existence in the Church. But the vows did create very strong and close bonds, directed to a specific apostolate 'which is most necessary',[44] namely the evangelization of the young of school age and preferably of the poor. If therefore we wish, in their regard, to use the word 'religious' correctly, we can in no way use it as a common noun but solely as a qualifying adjective (e.g., 'religious Brothers').

Chapter 6

The Gratuitous School

1. An ambiguous situation

By the heroic vow of 1691, followed by the perpetual vows and the election of 6 and 7 June 1694, which were their first fruits, the Society of the Christian Schools was now solidly structured internally. But outside, for all that, it remained unprotected. Possessing no official recognition, it could exist in a diocese only by the tolerance of its bishop and in a parish only with the agreement of its priest. The expression of the *Memoir on the Habit* 'at present this community is founded only on Providence'[1], is not to be read exclusively from the financial angle. It must he extended to the total domain of the life and activity of the Institute which would be dependent on the interplay of two authorities: that of the legitimate Superior who governed it and that of the local pastor who gave it hospitality. Until his death the Founder would always have this thorn in his flesh.

Expansion

M. Baudrand, after suffering a stroke, was replaced on 13 February by Joachim Trotti de la Chétardie. Having in keeping with the tradition of the parish a keen interest in the religious education of children, he added to the two schools already existing in the rue Princesse and the rue du Bac those of the rue St-Placide, on 2 October 1697, and of the rue Fosses-Monsieur-le-Prince, in October 1699.

Furthermore, de la Chétardie intervened in a personal way through two special foundations in May 1698, the boarding school for 'forty young Irish who had taken asylum in France from the persecution of Catholics in their native land'[2] and, towards the end of the same year, the Sunday School intended for 'two hundred students divided into various classes who were given instruction proper to their age and capacities. The least advanced learned how to read and write; the others were taught arithmetic; some learned drawing. This first class period which lasted two hours or so, was followed by the Catechism lesson, and this by a spiritual exhortation given by one of the Brothers. All doors of this school were open to all who presented themselves, provided they showed good will. Thus, none of these young men could excuse his ignorance of Christian doctrine and of the duties required for salvation, on the pretext that he had to earn his living during the week'.[3]

Towards the end of the same year 1698, another school was set up in rue Ourcine, in the faubourg St-Marcel, at the request of the parish priest of St-Hippolyte, Michel Lebreton. 'When he saw for himself how much benefit could derive from a gratuitous school conducted by disinterested and truly pious teachers, he looked even further afield and conceived the idea of extending to country parishes the blessings that the Lord was bestowing on his own'.[4] John Baptist de La Salle then proposed to him that the Training College for School Masters, which had so unhappily come to an end in Rheims, be re-established next to the school. He accepted and at the beginning of the following year it opened under the direction of Brother Nicholas Vuyart.

At the same time, the expansion of the Institute took it into the provinces. On 12 October 1699, two schools opened in Chartres and, in August 1700, another at Calais with Brother Gabriel Drolin as Director. Guillaume Samson-Bazin, born on 14 January 1682 in the parish of St-Séverin in Paris and who entered the Society on his eighteenth birthday, taking the name of Brother Timothy, was sent to Chartres in September 1702. He was suffering from a serious swelling on the knee. Before setting out he asked John Baptist to bless it and on arriving discovered that he was cured. On 3 April 1742, ten years before his death, he drew up a testimony to this miracle which is kept in the Archives of the Generalate.[5]

'The same year, 1702, M. De la Salle put into effect an idea with which God had long inspired him. This was to send to Rome two of his disciples to make an establishment there.'[6] He intended thus to make evident his attachment to the Church and the Pope, as he would later recall in his Will: 'I sent two Brothers to Rome to ask of God the grace that their Society would always remain completely submissive to it'.[7] Setting out on foot with a hundred francs to meet the expenses of a journey of two months, they had to pass through Lyons, cross the Alps by the Col de Frejus to arrive in Turin; then, by Piacenza and Modena, to reach the Papal States along the Adriatic coast. This was the least complicated route as far as passports were concerned. They arrived in November. One of them, 'the younger, returned to France some months after he had set out and he left behind his senior, named Gabriel Drolin, who persevered there for twenty-six years. This was not without his having at first to suffer great poverty and endure great difficulties'.[8]

Persecution

The two Brothers for whom John Baptist de La Salle had ensured the necessary training for managing the Sunday School decided that with this experience they could now aspire to a situation both more respectable and more remunerative. They left the Institute in 1702, thus bringing down this institution so dear to M. de La Chétardie.

He had devoted the great part of his personal resources to works of charity. The fourteen classes opened in his parish gave admittance to more than a thousand children. He was justly proud of this and he considered the Sunday School as the crowning of his pastoral achievement. He considered John Baptist to be responsible for its failure and he ever after nursed a grudge against him.

He had, besides, views very different from those of the Founder as to how to run the Institute. Contrary to Mgr le Tellier who wanted to limit the Lasallian enterprise to his own diocese of Rheims, M. de La Chétardie saw no problem with multiplying schools wherever they were asked for. But he wanted them to be under the sole authority of the parish priests, without any bonding between themselves, and freed from the structure of the Institute which included them and united them. Having succeeded in freeing the charitable schools from the control of the Grand Chantre,[9] he had no intention of submitting to any other. De La Salle, obviously, could not accept what would empty the Institution of all reality. But because other ecclesiastics in the circle of the Archbishop of Paris, Mgr de Noailles, shared the ideas of M. de la Chétardie, he felt that there was a growing tension which the least circumstance might cause to explode.

A sad story of excessive penances imposed by the Director of Novices on two of his subjects and of the too rigid discipline enforced by the Director of the schools, set fire to the gunpowder. The parish priest drew up for the Archbishop a memorandum in which 'without calling the pious Founder the author of his disciples' conduct, he blamed him for it and concluded that he should be deposed and someone else put in his place, someone with greater wisdom, better able to govern the Brothers and to take care of an Institute which was so useful to the Church'.[10] Mgr de Noailles, easily influenced, agreed and directed one of his Vicars General M. Pirot to announce to the Brothers that they had another Superior.

On Sunday 3 December 1702, he introduced to the community De La Salle's 'replacement', M. Bricot, a priest from Lyons. There was a great uproar. The Brothers, deeply attached to John Baptist de La Salle, bound to him by the association and the obedience which they had vowed, and aware that he was being 'changed only in order that the Rule be reformed and the Society be dissolved', unanimously refused. They wrote to the Brothers in the provinces who had their parish priests intervene. Finally, they threatened to abandon the schools, an argument to which M. de la Chétardie could not remain indifferent. Witness of their fidelity and aware of the insecurity of his own enterprises, he joined the mediators. On their side, in order to spare the feelings of the Archbishop, the Brothers declared they would accept M. Bricot on condition that his title would be considered purely honorific and that nothing in the Rule would be touched. The priest from Lyons had the good sense to withdraw. From this attack, the idea of association came out victorious, saved by the Brothers themselves.

2. The school in the Rue de Charonne

Its establishment

At their express request and with the hope of disarming his enemies by making them forget about him, John Baptist de La Salle transferred his community across the Seine to the east of Paris to the faubourg St-Antoine which was attached to the parish of St Paul. This house in the rue de Charonne, about four kilometres from the rue Princesse, was extremely cramped. It was not possible to receive all the Brothers there on Thursday or Sunday evenings or for the retreats in September. Close by, however, was the convent of the Filles de Sainte-Marguerite where the Founder was able to say Mass in their chapel.

On 20 July he brought his novitiate there. In October he opened a class which had as its signboard 'Brothers of the Christian Schools,' and finally in November he was able to set up the Sunday School which he had managed to re-open in April. He could do this because, although the Brothers to whom he had proposed the necessary studies had refused because it exposed them to the temptation to leave the Institute, he had succeeded in convincing one of them to overcome his concerns.

A lawsuit

Once again, the success of this school unleashed the anger of the Writing Masters. At the same time, the masters of the Little Schools, knowing the coolness of the parish priest towards De La Salle, denounced the latter before the Grand Chantre.

On 7 February as a result of the complaints of the Writing Masters, all the furniture, all the teaching material and even the signboard 'Brothers of the Christian Schools' were seized. On the 9th, De La Salle was summoned to appear at the Chatelet, the Central Court in Paris. On the 14th, the Grand Chantre renewed the prohibition against opening any school without his authorisation.

On the 22nd John Baptist was condemned by the court unless he taught only the poor who were recognized as such. This sentence brought about the closure of the Teaching College for country schoolmasters as well the school attached to it, directed by Brother Nicolas Vuyart in the parish of Saint-Martin.

On 19 March John Baptist appealed against the sentence of the Grand Chantre and on 4 May against the seizure of the school at rue de Charonne. In reply, the Writing Masters brought a new action, this time naming De La Salle and eighteen Brothers. On 11 July, all of these were condemned to pay a fine which was impossible for them to pay.

On 29 August, a final sentence of the Chatelet confirmed those of 22 February and 11 July. A notice to this effect was attached to the school door but the parents tore it off in the course of the day. This verdict recognized the right of the parish priests to have charity schools but refused the Brothers the right to live in community without having obtained official written approval. John Baptist could no longer retain in Paris the Brothers who had been condemned by name. In the following six months, he was obliged to disperse them in the country, to Chartres, Dijon, Rouen … On 26 September Nicolas Vuyart left the Institute. In October, the school in rue des Fossés Monsieur-le-Prince closed its doors. In December, the novices were brought back to rue Princesse.

What kind of gratuity for the school?

In order to indicate those responsible for the conflict which had such serious consequences for John Baptist, Blain writes:

> The schoolmasters declared war on him again with renewed fury, and this time successfully, because the parish priest of Saint Sulpice no longer shielded the Founder from their attacks. It was De La Chétardie who had given orders that the Christian Schools should admit indiscriminately all children who requested gratuitous instruction. His order was right ... But it was precisely the decision to admit to the Gratuitous Schools all the children who wished to enter that disturbed the Parisian schoolmasters.[11]

It is easy to understand that the charity school required no contribution from those attending it because they could not pay. But it was quite otherwise with the Christian school. Gratuity in this case came from the sole fact that it was the Brothers who refused any payment, no matter the financial situation of the parents.

Blain justifies this line of action by the difficulty of 'distinguishing in a great city the families which can afford to pay the teachers' fees from those that cannot'.[12] Once again, he is seeing the problem too narrowly for this was not the way in which John Baptist de La Salle saw it.

His faith showed him that the Christian school was directed to the salvation of children. This salvation is a free gift for everyone, whether they be rich or poor, for they all have the same natural inability to achieve it by themselves. 'The free gift of God is life eternal in Jesus Christ Our Lord' (Romans 6:23).

This attitude bespeaks a different concept of justice from that dispensed by the Chatelet! If the gratuity of the school had no other motivation than financial (as was the case with the charity schools), the Writing Masters would have been justified in excluding the better-off from it. Therefore, in ignoring the sentences passed against him and the Brothers, De La Salle could only feel himself in the right because his project was not driven by economic concerns.

The pastoral character of the Christian school was to incarnate the very divine gratuity itself! 'It is God alone who justifies us by his very goodness, he says in the *Duties of a Christian*.[13] In making their school free, the Brothers shared in God's gratuity 'who makes the sun rise on the good and the bad and allows the rain to fall on the just and the unjust' (Matthew 5:45).

'You have received freely: give freely' (Matthew 10:8). It is strange to note that the Founder never cites this clear and so radical Gospel passage, so appropriate for the Lasallian vocation. He prefers a passage from the first Letter to the Corinthians (9:18), which he makes use of twice in the *Meditations for the Time of Retreat*:

> Thank God who has had the goodness to employ you to procure such an important advantage for children. Be faithful and exact to do this without any payment, so that you can say with Saint Paul, the source of my consolation is to announce the Gospel free of charge, without having it cost anything to those who hear me (MTR 194 1).

> It was, then, the spread of God's glory by the preaching of the Gospel that made up all the consolation of this great apostle, and this must be yours as well, to make God and his Son Jesus Christ known to the flock confided to you. Oh! What glory for you to have this resemblance to that chosen vessel of election! With joy, then, say as he does, that the greatest cause of your joy in this life is to proclaim the Gospel free of charge, without it having it cost anything to those who hear it (MTR 207, 2).

Doubtless, John Baptist finds it more dynamising for the Brothers to link their apostolate to that of Saint Paul and so animate their zeal by his example. In any case, he defines the Institute in his Rule as 'a society in which profession is made to maintain schools gratuitously'[14] and he further stipulates that 'the Brothers everywhere keep schools gratuitously', adding that 'this is essential to their Institute'.[15]

On the one hand, he presents this school gratuity as a response to the abandoned condition of poor children, saying 'God has had the goodness to remedy so great a misfortune by the establishment of the Christian Schools, where the teaching is offered free of charge and entirely for the glory of God (MTR 194,1), and on the other as the fruit of the vows pronounced by the Brothers: 'You have committed yourself to keep schools gratuitously, and to live on bread alone if need be, rather than accept anything. Be on your guard, then, never to receive anything whatever, either from the students or from their parents' (Meditation 153,3).

Nowadays, establishments in the Lasallian network remain faithful to this value by defining themselves as 'schools open to all'. If, at the time of the

Founder, financial criteria was the point of discrimination, our 'exploded' society has seen plenty of other kinds of distinction: race, country, culture and religion. More than ever, then, it is for the Christian school to maintain the clear line of Lasallian gratuity and its enlargement by opposing every form of segregation or marginalisation. No one, indeed, is excluded from the proposal of salvation offered by God to all.

For what poor?

Vocabulary ...

When John Baptist De La Salle uses the word 'poor' (87 times as an adjective and 161 times as a noun) he gives it the then current meaning, without reference to any specific social group. The term, as we have already noted, does not appear in the vow formulas of 1691 and 1694 nor in the explanation given of them in the *Collection*.

The expression 'the poorest' is used twice only—'they will distribute bread to the poorest';[16] 'whether you have not neglected some students because they were the slowest, perhaps also the poorest'[17]—thus exclusively with reference to a clearly marked group, a class, and not in a generic sense as often today, for example in the current Rule: 'bringing his salvation to the least and to the poorest'.[18]

The expression 'especially the poor' is found only once: 'to have instructed children, especially the poor'.[19] It will come into general usage in the Institute after the first article of the Bull of Approbation of 1724: 'to teach children, especially poor children, those things which pertain to a good and Christian life'.[20] The Rule of 1987 uses formulas such as 'above all', 'especially' (articles 3 and 10, and 14 in the English version); 'preferential option in favour of the poor' (article 41).

Of the seventeen occurrences of the word 'artisan', the workers or working class, only one has reference to the school but in a key-phrase: 'how important it is for an artisan to know how to read and write well'.[21] The others, especially in his catechisms, refer to problems of Christian living: dispensation from fasting prohibition of some works on Sundays, the confession of sins referring to one's work

As for the expression 'artisans and the poor', it is typical of the Founder and highly significant. Two instances appear in the *Rules of Decorum and Christian Politeness* in the chapter dealing with types of entertainment which are not open to them:

— there are those which are only available to the rich such as balls, dances and plays;

— there are others which are more usual among artisans and the poor;[22]

— there are those in which it is only the artisans and the poor who ordinarily take part.[23]

The other five instances appear in foundation texts, the *Rule* and the *Meditations for the Time of Retreat*:

— artisans and the poor being ordinarily little instructed (RC 2,4);

— to procure this advantage for the children of the working class and of the poor (RC 2,5);

— disorders among the working class and the poor (2,6);

— a practice which is only too common for the working class and the poor (MTR 194,1);

— piety is increased among the faithful, especially among the working class and the poor (MTR 207,3).

De La Salle's intention

Thus John Baptist included in the same category the poor man who had no resources other than those of charity and the artisan who had for his daily support only what the work of each day brought in. At different times he was himself to experience a similar situation. He confided this to Brother Gabriel Drolin when he wrote to him on 4 September 1705, 'I have to count up my resources by the day'.[24] We use the expression 'to live from day to day'. Our problem is not to know whether in reality artisans and the poor make up two different social groups but to understand why, in the thinking of the Founder, they constitute only one: those who will benefit from his school. One would think that this joining of the two classes is obvious.

De La Salle has a will towards openness

John Baptist did not act in the manner of the royal power which put the poor in its General Refuges nor like the Church authority which listed them in its Registers. He set up no dividing line between those who, in their degree and their own way, shared the same difficulties and the same needs. He wished also to give his Brothers the widest possible scope in intending his schools for all those who could profit by them, no matter what might be their special situations. His vision was not restricted as it would be if it were to welcome only those who were most deprived and rejected. Even if degrees of hardship and misery do exist, there are no categories within the Lasallian charism.

De La Salle takes into account not only the financial situation

The evil which John Baptist de La Salle identified and which he set out to fight was not material poverty as such but one of its particularly destructive effects which he calls 'abandonment'. This moral misery, which consists especially in the absence of human formation, has its cause not only in the lack of money but even more in religious ignorance and the loss of educational direction because of the accumulation of earthly cares. Even if it touches first of all the children of the poor, one can also meet it in more wealthy situations.

De La Salle and the Brothers express a specific commitment

To this evil De La Salle, with his Brothers, brought a suitable reponse, namely the gratuitous Christian school. Through it, he aimed to offer a remedy for all educational shortcomings: intellectual, professional, social, moral, religious. He did not restrict himself to a simple philanthropic gesture of the type: 'If you give a poor man a fish, he will eat today; if you teach him to fish, he will eat every day'. This dimension, which exists in his work and which some have wanted to retain on its own, takes its place in a project of a *pastoral* nature which gives it its true meaning and which also assures it its fullness.

An axis of reference

In practice, the expression 'the artisans and the poor' offered the Directors of the schools a general rule when enrolling pupils, one not to be taken strictly literally but to be applied without any exclusiveness.

5. True charity

A text in De La Salle's catechism, *The Duties of a Christian*, throws strong light on this consideration: 'There are two classes of almsgiving: the one corporal which serves to draw the poor man out of the want and misery he suffers in regard to his body, the other spiritual when one brings comfort to one's neighbour in his spiritual miseries and needs. Not all men are in a position to give their goods to the poor but all can help them spiritually by contributing to their salvation whether by their own good example or by obtaining for them or actually giving them instruction: it is to this that pastors are especially obligated as are all those who have the responsibility of instructing others and of working for their salvation and their sanctification'.[25]

'The poor you have always with you' (John 12:8). 'Every day you are with the poor.'[26]

Lasallian Texts

Abandonment

[The following texts of De La Salle are sociological statements which have the authority of someone who speaks of things that were evident to him. Editor].

All disorders, especially among the working class and the poor, usually arise from their having been in childhood left to themselves and badly brought up. It is almost impossible to repair this evil at a more advanced age, because the bad habits they have acquired are overcome only with great difficulty, and scarcely ever entirely, no matter what care may be taken to destroy them whether by frequent instructions or the use of the Sacraments. As the principal fruit to be expected from the institution of the Christian schools is to forestall these disorders and prevent their evil consequences, it is easy to conceive the importance of such schools and their necessity.[27]

… these children, a great number of whom would otherwise be abandoned … [28]

… they have to abandon their children to themselves.[29]

… if they are abandoned to their own will, they will run the risk of ruining themselves … [30]

… Will you then abandon them and leave them without any instruction? [31]

… You should look upon the children whom you are charged to teach as poor abandoned orphans; in fact, though the majority of them do have a father on earth they are still as if they had none and are abandoned to themselves for the salvation of their souls; this is the reason God places them as if under your guardianship ... [32]

Causes of children's situation of abandonment

On the part of parents generally:

— **Religious ignorance**: most parents are not sufficiently enlightened in these matters;[33]
— **For the rich, the management of their family inheritance**: some are taken up with their daily concerns and the care of their family;[34]
— **For the poor, the overburden of work**: others are under the constant anxiety of earning the necessities of life for themselves and their children.[35]

On the part of artisans and the poor:

— **Religious ignorance**: the working class and the poor being usually little instructed;[36]
— **The overburden of work**: being occupied all day in gaining a livelihood for themselves and their children;[37]
— **Being obliged to look for work** outside their homes;[38]
— **Poverty**: their poverty does not allow them to pay teachers.[39]

Consequences for all concerned

For the parents:

— their inability to impart moral and religious education;
— they cannot take the time to teach their children their duties as Christians;[40]
— they cannot give their children the needed instruction or a suitable Christian Education, a failure to exercise their parental duties;[41]
— they have to abandon their children to themselves; allow them to live on their own, roaming all over like vagabonds as long as they are not able to put them out to some work; [42]
— their indifference as to the children's schooling: they have no concern to send their children to school.[43]

For the children:

— lack of moral and religious formation: 'the children who come to you either have not had any instruction, or have been taught the wrong things';[44]

— bad habits: 'these poor children accustomed to lead an idle life for many years, have great difficulty in adjusting when it comes time for them to go to work';[45]

— the bad habits they have acquired are overcome only with difficulty, and scarcely ever entirely, no matter what care may be taken to destroy them;[46]

— bad companions: through association with bad companions they learn to commit many sins which later are very difficult to stop because of the persistent bad habits they have contracted over such a long time;[47] if they have received some good lessons, bad companions or their own bad habits have prevented them from benefiting.[48]

Inadequacies in the education of the poor

— Parents either neglect to send their children to school or do not take much trouble to make them come or be assiduous. This difficulty is quite common among the poor.[49] They are indifferent to school, persuaded that their children learn very little, or for some other trifling objection.

— the means of remedying the negligence of the parents, especially of the poor.

— the harm that may be done their children by lack of instruction in those things which concern their salvation, with which the poor are often little concerned. [50]

— this class of poor are ordinarily those who receive alms.

— ordinarily the children of the poor do as they wish. Their parents often take no care of them or even idolize them. What their children want they also want.[51]

— it is a practice only too common for the working class and the poor to allow their children to live on their own, roaming all over like vagabonds as long as they are not able to put them to some work; these parents have no concern to send their children to school.[52]

— be prepared to endure abuse, outrages, and calumnies in return for all the good you have tried to do for others. This is the main reward that God promises and often the only one we receive from the poor in recompense for the good we do for them;[53]

— the only thanks you should expect for instructing children especially the poor is abuse, insult, calumny, persecution and even death.[54]

Chapter 7

To be or not to be a Brother

1. The Normandy heritage

Darnétal

In September 1704, at Darnétal, a large market town a league from Rouen, occurred the death of Jean Haudoul, a disciple of Father Nicolas Barré. He had been employed as a teacher by Adrien Nyel. To fill this position, the Marian Congregation, a society of lay people who among other good works managed the charity school, contacted John Baptist de La Salle. As intermediary they used a Rouen parish priest who during his seminary days at Saint Sulpice had seen the school in rue Princesse in action. The founder replied on 26 September:

> I learned from Father Chardon this morning that you had written to him asking for some of our Brothers for Rouen, that you would like to have two and want to know how much will be needed to maintain them. I am quite ready to send you two. As regards the cost, you know we are not very hard to please, but we cannot send you one only ... I think that we will easily come to an agreement and that the Brothers I send will give satisfaction.[1]

They arrived at Darnétal at the beginning of February 1705 and 'they proved very exact in fulfilling the obligations of their state, as well as giving careful attention to the education of the children who had been confided to their care ... The Archbishop was soon aware of the success of the schools ...

and sure of the good that would result decided to invite the Brothers to take over the poor schools of the city of Rouen which had been started by Adrien Nyel some years before along the lines of Father Barré's thinking'.[2]

That did not meet with the approval of the teachers who taught in them any more than with the Administrators who regulated them. Blain analysed the situation perceptively, writing that the disapproval 'may have been prejudice against new organisations; or apprehension on seeing an unknown Community taking its place in a city which believed itself oversupplied by the number it already had; or distrustful lest they lose their acquired right to nominate subjects for these schools as a kind of benefice; or antipathy and secret aversion for strangers'.[3]

Archbishop Colbert had to find a compromise, and when John Baptist appeared before the Rouen Bureau he found their conditions more stringent than the previous ones, which had already been very severe. He accepted them, 'for he had long had a premonition that God had destined him to take over the schools founded by Nyel for whom he had maintained special affection since the time when they had worked together establishing those of Rheims and the surrounding towns'.[4] Besides, as he saw that his novitiate could not long stand up to the continual troubles raised against it in Paris, he was hopeful that he might be able to transfer it to this new setting in Rouen.

Rouen

Leaving Paris on foot on 15 May the Brothers reached Rouen on the 19th, at the end of a journey which, under the direction of De La Salle, was transformed into a retreat with silence, prayer and the performance of the community exercises. They were taken on trial and lodged in the General Hospital where able-bodied poor to the number of five or six hundred were looked after.

Their duties began with the dawn.

> The Brothers were assiduous in getting the paupers up and having them say their morning prayers. About eight o'clock, four of them went off to their classes. They came back at noon, served the paupers at table and kept watch to make them observe order during the meal. Then they themselves ate, after which they went back to school. Returning to the Hospital around six in the evening, they took the paupers to the refectory and ended the day with them as they had begun it, by having them say their prayers.[5]

The school of St-Maclou, overlooking the parish cemetery, functioned immediately with one Brother. The teacher who was already employed there kept his job. Previously, in rue Princesse, John Baptist de La Salle had kept the trade teacher Rafrond on the staff for several months.

The school of St-Godard occupied the Gogelin Tower, a remnant of the old ramparts. Today it has disappeared, but the Joan of Arc Tower which is still standing and accessible is proof of the unhygienic and squalid conditions which the Brothers and pupils had to endure.

The Brother who taught at the Hospital was no better off with regard to filth, noise and continual movement.

Finally, at the beginning of August, two Brothers took over the schools of St-Éloi and St-Vivien. In each of the classes the number of students was in excess of one hundred.

Saint-Yon

John Baptist having, as was his custom, consulted the Archbishop about the eventual transfer of his novitiate to Rouen, Archbishop Colbert recommended a former manor house flanked by a chapel, in the centre of a nine hectare property. It was located in the St Sever area, on the left bank of the Seine. Its last owner, Eustache de St-Yon, master of the Chamber of Finance in Normandy, had bequeathed it his name. The rental agreement was signed in Paris on 11 July 1705, and by mid-August the novices had moved in. For Director they had Brother Barthélemy, 'a wise man with a gentle disposition', and for Sub-Director Brother Dominique Scellier. He was born at Villiers-le-Bel, north of Paris, and was the youngest of a family of five children, four of whom were boys. He entered the Institute in 1701, a year after his eldest brother. He found amongst the novices the other two brothers as well as his father. The latter subsequently fulfilled the duties of porter at St-Yon, and died tired out in 1713 while making his way on foot to Guise, where he had been sent as cook. Meanwhile he had seen Dominique die of a debilitating illness, on 16 June 1706, at the age of 23. Blain tells the charming story of this family in 'A summary of the lives of some Brothers', published as an appendix to his biography of De La Salle.[6]

At the same time, the Founder made a gratuitous school available for the poor children of the parish of St-Sever. Here the novices added to their spiritual formation a practical initiation into pedagogy.

The Boarding School

Its creation

To cover the costs involved in all of this, De La Salle persuaded himself that 'God, in order to provide for our subsistence wanted us to take in boarding pupils at low cost and to give them a sound education and a good upbringing'.[7] The Bursar at St-Yon who confided this to Blain completed it as follows:

> By doing that you will gain the affection and esteem of the people of that town where so far you have not been shown any. You may still have to suffer a little but it will not last long. Meanwhile, be sure that God will give you what is necessary to live, if you serve him well.[8]

So from the month of October onwards, John Baptist opened his house to several young people from Rouen and its environs.

> They are in the care of a Brother who keeps an eye on them all the time, and who teaches them reading, writing and arithmetic. Those who so desire, and who can, learn drawing, geometry and architecture.[9]

Certainly there was no Latin, not because of the fact that the Brothers were forbidden to study it, but because the Founder saw the education of these boys who came from bourgeois surroundings from the same point of view as he saw that of 'children of artisans and the poor'. It was to be an apprenticeship as practical and as complete as possible for their future as adults in the area, not of manual trades, but in their case of callings in industry and commerce. He did all this always with the same pastoral purpose, believing that to assure for a young man, together with a knowledge of religion, a suitable human position, was to give him an effective means of working at his salvation.

Its value

This establishment is rightly looked upon as the starting point in France of what, one hundred and sixty years later, would be known as secondary modern education. The Lasallian tradition can make that claim with good reason, rejoice in it and feel a legitimate pride in it.

On no account must we distort the action of John Baptist de La Salle and see in him only an audacious innovator in the educational field. In initiating this revolutionary path, he did not act as a pedagogue intent on improving the school institution to make it better adapted to its purpose. He acted as a zealous pastor, determined to bring to the school from within whatever transformation was necessary to make it Christian, that is, to make the school a place where the Gospel is announced and above all accepted because it has become part of life.

Of course, this pedagogical system, which he brought into being in this attempt to christianize the school, has a value in itself which it keeps even if it is used 'for its own sake', without its original religious purpose. On how many occasions has the proclamation of the Good News produced a fortunate humanitarian fall-out from which society has profited while laicising it. Drawing up a list of examples would be to unfold the history of our civilisation in its most significant moments.

For us today, rejoicing in the good already accomplished and longing for the good remaining to be achieved through all the forms of commitment which we are experiencing in the furrow of the Founder, we know that he desired to give to his undertakings no other direction than a pastoral one. We know that remaining faithful to him means nourishing in our hearts his zeal for the salvation of youth.

Its extension

The new style of college was so successful with the well-off families in the area that they did not hesitate to enrol in it 'problem boys', dubbed by Blain 'unmanageable and perverted young men'.[10] A special section was opened for them in 1706. Here they received the same formation in a framework of discipline and added supervision. A third establishment, called a 'reformatory', was started to receive young delinquents. 'Confirmed criminals were consigned there, some by decrees of parliament, others by court orders and several by authority of their parents ... It is hardly believable how many really perverse men have been converted in this house; how many rebellious and unmanageable children there lost their belligerence and impiety; how many others began to walk once more in the path of salvation and duty ... A few even asked to receive the Brothers' habit and became members of the Institute.'[11]

St-Yon thus became a centre of pedagogical and educational research. Its renown became so widespread that the followers of De La Salle acquired the nickname 'Yontain Brothers ' which the malice of Voltaire corrupted to 'ignorant Brothers ' (from the similar sound in French of the word *ignorantins* Editor).

A different practice of gratuity

A preliminary question

It is curious to note that St-Yon seems to have left fewer traces in the Lasallian imagination than the school for the Irish introduced in the preceding chapter. If one, like Épinal, illustrates the relationships of the Founder with the mighty of this world, the other shows his connections with the wealthy class from which he sprang but which he left. These connections prompt the following question: in Rheims, De La Salle aimed his schools at those without means of support; in Paris he admitted, together with the poor, some pupils able to pay; now, in Rouen, he offers to the bourgeoisie a college endowed with a boarding school. Is there not some backsliding here? It is a real question and one that cannot be ignored, all the more because the school for the Irish resulted from a proposition made from outside and represented only an anecdotal phenomenon in his life, while the boarding school at St-Yon was the fruit of his personal initiative and constituted, during his latter years, an outstanding achievement, a side of his work structurally as significant as the Training College for country teachers.

Handling the pastoral care of the poor

Material for understanding his motivation can be found in the correspondence he kept up at this time with Brother Gabriel Drolin who had been living in Rome since 1702 and whose situation was even more precarious than that of his Superior. Already, in 1704, when Gabriel was living with a trader of French origin and who accepted as payment for his board the lessons in reading and writing Drolin gave to his two young daughters, De La Salle, in a letter dated 13 August, had reminded him, 'You must not try to cut down on expenses by doing what is contrary to your Institute practices … I beg you, do nothing that is not in accord with your Institute, whatever the cost, otherwise God will not bless you (that is, God will not give spiritual fruitfulness to your work).'[12] He ended his letter by coming back insistently to this obligation: 'Above all else, do not do anything that is not in accord with your Institute'.[13]

A year later Gabriel had left this lodging. He was living in a two-room apartment, using one room as a bedroom and the other as a classroom where he taught a few destitute children. His less than minimum income left him problems at the end of each month. He conveyed to the Founder, whose rent for St-Yon (400 livres per year) had dried up his resources and who responded on 4 September 1705, '... if you rely on me entirely right now, you will place me in an awkward position, since I am less able to help you than I have ever been ... I have established our novitiate in a fine house in a suburb of Rouen ... That is why I am short of money. You ought not to have gone into debt without getting my approval beforehand ... Since then I have negotiated the arrangements at Rouen, and it has drained me of money ...'[14]

As he felt very strongly about living on credit he came back to the question to better hammer in the nail:

> Please do not go into debt without my approval, for I am not at all happy about debts. I do not want any and have never wanted or allowed any in our communities. There is nothing I detest so much. That is why you will never be able to count on me again when it comes to debts, for I will not listen to the least suggestion. As far as expenditure goes, I want to look ahead not behind me.[15]

At the same time, he touches on a religious theme dear to him, abandonment to Providence:

> I know it is better to live in more difficult circumstances, withdrawn from all worldly concerns, and I am glad that you are in such dispositions. Still, when you decide to do this, you must put yourself in the hands of Divine Providence, or, if you have not enough virtue for that nor enough faith, then you must take the necessary means before you carry out your plan. If you do neither, you are not acting as a Christian nor as an intelligent man'.[16]

He repeated this advice in his next letter dated 28 October:

> I am well aware that it is advantageous to live withdrawn from the world, but you have to have life's necessities, and you need to know where you can get them before you leave the world. [17]

'This maxim is really the finest of human wisdom', would comment the theologian charged with examining the writings of John Baptist de La Salle in 1849, 'but it does not at all breathe that complete confidence that a man of God places in Divine Providence. Let there be no thought of the morrow in abandoning oneself to God, and God will provide for everything, such is the spirit of the saints'.[18] We note that the Church has canonized the Founder and not the Devil's Advocate!

And the rich?

Such 'pastoral management' principles presided over the birth of St-Yon and they did not lead to any compromise with wealth but purely an implied active sympathy of those who have for the benefit of those who have not.

The feelings the Founder experienced towards the rich were conformable with those of Christ himself and expressed with equal vigour: 'Woe to you who are rich, for you have received your consolation'.[19] 'It is easier for a camel to go through the eye of a needle than for someone who is rich to enter the kingdom of God.'[20] When references are missing he is not afraid to extrapolate, 'Jesus Christ did not say the Gospel is preached to the rich, but to the poor'[21] or again, 'this made him say to the disciples of John who asked him what they should tell their master: "Tell him", replied the Saviour, "that I preach the Gospel to the poor"'.[22]

His preferential option for the latter does not entail any ambiguity. It is as radical as it is definitive. He does not envisage his own life nor that of the Brothers as other than one of service to the poor. However, neither prejudice nor exclusivism can be found in his conduct. Hospitable to all, like Christ, he did not show 'partiality to anyone' (Luke 20:21). If it happened that one of his works profited the rich in one way or another, he was not satisfied that it should bring no detriment to the poor. He was careful, on the contrary, that in the first place it furthered their greatest good.

Destined for the salvation of the poor, the Institute seeks that result by working at their advancement. That of the rich is not within its ambit, does not fit its aims, does not concern it. Despite the pressure to get it to bend to the interests of the rich that the power of money exercises on it and will continue to exercise on it, it has to preserve its independence at all costs, to remain true to its charism by its extension of the gratuity which the Founder declared to be essential for it. It is in this spirit that after at first thinking of soliciting charity from the rich for his schools, De La Salle is now making them pay for work done for them but of which the ultimate beneficiaries remain, in reality, the poor.

2. Extreme poverty still and always

The General Hospital

In Paris the bullying tactics of the writing masters started up again in October 1705, and in 1706 the Brothers found themselves forced to abandon their schools and could not open them at the beginning of October. Meanwhile in Rouen the situation was becoming untenable. Worn out by two years of grinding work which took all their time and strength, the Brothers ended up addressing a collective memorandum to De La Salle in June 1707 (that is, after two years!):

> In their document the Brothers brought out clearly how necessary it was to get them out of the Hospital, where the spirit of their Institute ran as much risk as their health did. The advantage to the poor as well as their own required it. Nor was it difficult for them to prove their case: 1. Since they were too few in proportion to the number of students, they could not do a good job. 2.The classes were too big, the teachers were overworked, and many of the children were neglected. 3. Overwork affected not only the teachers' health, but discipline, order, silence and instruction itself; in a word the purpose of the schools could not be attained. 4. Fatigue, the multiplicity of their tasks, and the long hours caused disorder in their interior life, so that they had no time for mental prayer and their other exercises of piety.
>
> The conclusion was that they should leave the Hospital, find a house in the city and live there according to the spirit of the Institute. They added that if the administrators were willing to give them the income of the capital destined to provide for the teachers of the city's gratuitous schools, they would be content with these modest appointments. It would then be possible to increase the number of Brothers so as to do the schoolwork properly. They feared less to suffer from poverty than to be wanting in regularity.[23]

Previously, but in different circumstances, the Brothers had proceeded in a similar way to point out to their Father a serious problem or to suggest an initiative. Wishing only to govern with them, from the very beginning he had got them used to broad freedom in speaking their minds. He liked to listen to them and took great notice of their advice. So he transmitted their request to the Office of the Poor. It was accepted on 2 August.

> When the Brothers left, their work would be diminished by half, and some relief would be given to them; but the first condition was that their number should be doubled: ten Brothers were asked for to run the schools at Saint Maclou, Saint Vivien, Saint Godard and Saint Éloi. The second condition required of De La Salle was that he be satisfied with half the revenue from the foundation, namely 600 livres a year. If he agreed to these conditions, they would consent to let him run the schools in question. De La Salle agreed to everything, even though he was being asked for a great deal and was offered little or nothing in return.[24]

On 20 September the Brothers left the General Hospital and the former teachers took up their work again. John Baptist lodged the community in a small house in the parish of St-Nicolas. They lived there for five years in extreme destitution.

The reasons for lack of productivity

Blain has not kept for us the exact wording of this memoir but at least he has respected its tenor. In a simple and clear-sighted way the Brothers analysed their failure. They lay the blame on the flagrant disproportion between the task set and the human resources available. The physical fatigue, nervous tension and the ceaseless worry resulting from it, undermined their health as well as their spiritual life, at one stroke depriving their labour of a great part of its pastoral efficacy. That is what they deplored in stating that 'the fruitfulness of the schools was suffering', and that is what they wanted to remedy, 'to be able to run them fruitfully'. This colourful expression, repeated within a couple of lines, reveals the ambition close to their hearts. They wanted to procure for their pupils access to a good which was not confined to this earth, but which through it and beyond it aimed at heaven itself.

'Let the school be run well'

To express the same plan and the same expectation, John Baptist de La Salle made use of an expression which is found only in his correspondence. This leads to the supposition that it belongs to his spoken language, not to his written language. Letters to several Directors between 1705 and 1710 go through its variations in one form or another. 'Nothing must be left undone to ensure that the classes make progress.'[25] 'Take care that the classes run well. I will do my best to support your efforts.'[26] 'I am pleased that your school is progressing well and that you have plenty of students. Be sure to teach them well.'[27]

Sentences like these in which the expression appears in isolation do not allow us to clarify the exact meaning. We could allow ourselves to claim that it simply means that the school be well organized, that it guide the student to good results, a worthwhile formation and acceptable certificates.

Fortunately, other expressions are more explicit. 'Since you ask it, I will see that you have plenty of students. Be keen on carrying out your school duties, but please be as keen about your spiritual exercises as you are about class.'[28] 'Take care that your school runs well and that your community is faithful to the Rule.'[29] 'Your spiritual exercises and your school require all your care. If you involve yourself in anything else, you are acting in opposition to the designs of God.'[30]

But the most significant was written to Brother Mathias on 13 April 1708:

> You must not only carry out your class duties, but also the exercises, for class-work without the spiritual exercises will not do.[31]

What does it all mean? How does the effort which the Brothers make to lead a Christian life affect the usefulness of the Lasallian school? It is precisely that the school sees itself as Christian and pursues a supernatural end, namely the conversion and sanctification of its students. If the school institution is viewed only in its social function of teaching and human education, it is sufficient for the teacher to be competent and upright. But if an apostolic aim is attached to the school it is necessary for it to be Christian as well. It is only to the extent that teachers themselves live the Gospel that they will be able to be model for their disciples of the thinking of the children of God, of what the Founder calls 'the spirit of Christianity'. The expression occurs eight times in the *Meditations for the Time of Retreat*. Here is a sample:

> It is not enough that children be kept in school for most of the day and be kept busy. Those who have dedicated themselves to instruct them must devote themselves especially to bring them up in the Christian spirit, which gives children the wisdom of God that none of the princes of his world have known. It is completely opposed to the spirit and wisdom of the world, for which we must inspire children with a great horror since it serves as a cloak for sin. Children cannot be too much separated from such a great evil, because this alone can make them displeasing to God (*MTR* 194, 2).

The expression 'the school without the exercises does not run well' sends us back to the article of the *Memoir on the Habit*, 'the obligations of community life and their school duties demand their entire life and energy'.[32] Let us translate it as: A man whose spiritual life and apostolic life are one and the same. If the constraints of school tasks are such that they no longer allow the Brothers to be open to intimacy with Christ, what is the point of wearing out their strength in them: the game is not worth the candle. The experience in the General Hospital in Rouen, sadly, demonstrated it brilliantly.

Certainly a school must reach many criteria to attain and maintain the summit of its task. But what, definitely, made the heart of John Baptist de La Salle rejoice when he recognized that a school was running well, was not that it fulfilled these indispensable conditions, but that the smooth running that flowed from them enabled it to attain its pastoral aim of making its students 'good Christians'. That was the only result that counted in his eyes.

May God grant to the whole Lasallian network the same assessment as the Founder in the case of Avignon in his letter of 11 February 1705, to Brother Gabriel Drolin, 'The schools are making fine progress in Avignon'.[33]

Lasallian Texts

Fruit in the Lasallian ministry

1. All the good you are able to do in your work for those entrusted to you will be true and effective only insofar as Jesus Christ gives it his blessing and as you remain united with him. It is the same for you as for the branch of the vine, which can bear fruit only if it remains attached to the stem and draws its sap and strength from the vine ... The more your work for the good of your disciples is given life by him and draws its power from him, the more it will produce good in them.[34]

2. Teach them these truths not with learned words, lest the cross of Christ, the source of our sanctification, become void of meaning and all you say to them would produce no fruit in their minds or hearts.[35]

3. The same thing is true of those who instruct others. They are only the voice of the One who really disposes hearts to accept Jesus Christ and his holy teaching. The one who disposes them, according to Saint Paul, can only be God, who imparts to humans the gift of speaking of him ... Let us then humble ourselves, considering that we are nothing but a voice, and that of ourselves we cannot say anything that will do the least good for souls or make any impression on them, for we are a mere voice.[36]

4. Your zeal for the children you instruct would not go very far and would not have much result or success if it limited itself only to words. To make it effective it is necessary that your example support your instructions, and this is one of the main signs of your zeal.[37]

5. Virtue cannot hide. When it is seen it is attractive, and the example it gives makes such a strong impression on those who witness it practised or who hear it talked about that most people are led to imitate it. Is this the effect that your good behaviour and piety produce in your students? It is the main means you should use to win them over to God.[38]

6.Their perseverance in piety will be a great cause of consolation for you when you call to mind the result of their faith and of your instruction.[39]

7.Consider, then, that your reward in heaven will be all the greater as you will have accomplished more good in the souls of the children who are entrusted to your care.[40]

The practice of prayer

8. We can love God only while possessing his grace which makes us agreeable to him. This grace is given us only through prayer and the sacraments (*Duties of a Christian*, p. 300, 0, 10).

9. Prayer disposes us to tend to God, to raise ourselves to him and to unite ourselves intimately with him by conforming our affections to his so as to no longer wish for anything nor desire anything except him or what relates to him (*idem*, p. 401, 1, 4).

10. This is what Saint Chrysostom says: prayer is the light of our souls which it enlightens just as the sun lights up our bodies; it is the life of the soul and the one who does not pray assiduously is dead.
(*idem*, p. 401, 2, 5)

11. What we obtain best by prayer is either the knowledge or the love of God or some grace which helps us to acquire one or the other.
(*idem*, p. 402, 1, 9)

12. Prayer being an exercise beyond the natural powers of human beings, they need the Spirit of God within them to animate them and lead them in prayer.
(*idem*, p. 401, 1, 4)

13. When you pray to God, then, let it be with such deep humility that God will not be able to refuse you anything you ask.[41]

14. Prayer has little efficacy if it is not strengthened by mortification.[42]

15. We learn to speak to God only by listening to him; for to know how to speak to God and to converse with him can only come from God who has his own language which is special to him and which he shares only with his friends and confidants, to whom he gives the happiness of frequently conversing with him. [43]

Chapter 8

Faith shown
in zeal

1. The spirit of state

We have already pointed out that, as Blain has recorded in the *Memoir* of
June 1707, the word 'fruit' appears twice, once in a context of a negative past
period (the fruit [success] of the school suffered from it) and again in a context redolent of a positive future period ('in order to be able to manage the
schools fruitfully'). Similarly for an even more significant expression, namely
'the spirit of their Institute'. There is evidently a logical connection between
these two expressions since the school bears fruit only if the Brothers animate it according to the spirit of the Institute. Blain tells us, moreover, that
it was in pursuit of rediscovering this spirit and living by it that the brothers
asked to be allowed to leave the Bureau des Invalides (General Hospital)
where the spirit of the Institute was as at much risk as was their health.[1] They
indicated they were prepared to undergo all sacrifices, even to the extent of
'enduring poverty' which indeed was not lacking.

It does seem, however, that in writing 'the spirit of their Institute' the
biographer intended only what John Baptist de La Salle calls 'the spirit of
your state'. Thus we read in the Founder's writings among other quotations,
the following:

> If you truly possess the spirit of your state, God will make you discover in it
> all sorts of consolations, and even in your suffering (*Meditations*, 109, 2).

> Often meditate on the words of Holy Scripture to encourage yourself to do what is right and to be guided by the spirit of your state (*Meditations*, 192, 2).

> Ask God to renew in you ... the spirit of your state and profession (*Meditations*, 92, 3).

> Jesus Christ is in the midst of the Brothers in their exercises to imbue them with the spirit of their state and to strengthen and foster this spirit among them which spirit is the means and pledge of their salvation when preserved in its purity and entirety.[2]

What then is that state that is so important in the eyes of the Founder? Quite simply it is the state of being 'Brother', of being a man who has professed before God,

> I promise to unite myself and to remain in society with the Brothers of the Christian Schools who are associated to conduct together and by association schools for the service of the poor (Rule of 1987, article 25).

By means of this consecration, the Brother participates in a mission of the Church which gives him in the midst of the people of God, before ever his canonical status has been given official recognition, a unique position to which the word 'state' is doubly suited. This is so because the word 'state' includes both the distinctiveness of a social situation and the practice of a profession.

This 'state' confers on him, under the name of Brother, a definitive character at the same time as it commits him to a specific and a special way of living, binding him to an intense union with God in the apostolic activity totally directed to the salvation of his students.[3] All this conforms to the synthesis set out in article 10 of the *Mémoiré sur l'habit*, which must never be lost sight of, and to which we must constantly refer in order to perceive what constitutes the ideal type of Brother. In a further text we read as follows:

> Let all your time, following the example of Saint Martin, be spent in these two things: asking God insistently for the salvation of those who are under your guidance and seeking and helping them use these means (*Meditations*, 189,3).

'The spirit of our state' then, leads the Brothers to try to maintain, throughout the differing circumstances of their daily lives, the essential unity of their lives, convinced that any supernatural good they do depends completely on God. In this they hold sentiments similar to that which the Church evokes in praying the words of the evening office for the Thursday after the Ascension:

> Thou who didst pray in the Spirit to accomplish the work of the Father, grant to thy servants the spirit of prayer so that their work may also be Thine.

But when the Founder himself speaks of 'the Spirit of the Institute' he has in mind a spiritual reality which is at one and the same time more elevated and profound, more universal and even more necessary, and of which 'the spirit of our state' represents only one effect of the spirit of the Institute.

2. The spirit of the Institute

Let us examine this text which the Founder placed at the head of Chapter 2 of the Rule, when he set about making a revision in 1717, two years before his death:

> That which is of the utmost importance, and to which the greatest attention should be given in an Institute, is that all who compose it possess the spirit peculiar to it; that the novices apply themselves to acquire it, and that those who are already members, make it their first care to preserve and increase it in themselves: for it is this spirit that should animate all their actions, be the motive of their whole conduct: and those who do not possess it and those who have lost it, should be looked upon as dead members, and they should look upon themselves as such; because they are deprived of the life and grace of their state; and they should be convinced that it will be very difficult for them to preserve the grace of God.[4]

These are serious words, venerated like a family treasure, and placed as a prologue to the 1987 Rule, which it enlightens and animates.

The text goes on to explain:

> The Spirit of this Institute is first, a spirit of faith, which should lead those who compose it not to look upon anything but with the eyes of faith, not to do anything but in view of God, and to attribute all to God.[5]

> Secondly, the spirit of their Institute consists in an ardent zeal for the instruction of children, and for bringing them up in the fear of God.[6]

If, for the sake of clarity, we treat of the Spirit of faith and of zeal separately, as the Founder himself did, we regard it as incontestable that, in the ordinary run of our lives, these two elements of faith and zeal constitute one unified dynamic principle, which, to emphasize its synthesis we have taken the liberty to call 'a faith that begets zeal'.

3. The spirit of faith

Faith in action

The Founder returns, time and again, in his catechisms, meditations and other writings to the very important text in the epistle of Saint James 'faith without good deeds is useless' (James 2:26). This insistence is evidence enough that he cannot be satisfied with a faith that is purely speculative, an arid and purposeless contemplation of the divine mysteries revealed in Sacred Scriptures. For him this virtue of faith attains its end only when it is incarnated in a life and commitment within the People of God; that is to say when it becomes pastoral:

> It is especially in your actions that your faith should be seen by performing them only with the spirit of faith, as you are obliged according to the spirit of your Institute (*Meditations*, 147, 3).

> Be convinced that you will contribute to the good of the Church in your ministry only insofar as you have the fullness of faith and are guided by the spirit of faith which is the spirit of your state by which you should be animated (*Meditations*, 139, 2).

Even if he often described 'the spirit of the Institute' by the condensed expression 'spirit of faith', there can be no doubt that he includes also the virtue of zeal, as he explains in Chapter 2 of the Rule.[7] The present edition of the Rule 1987 restates in its article 7: 'The spirit of faith kindles in the Brothers an ardent zeal for those confided to their care in order to open their hearts to receive the salvation revealed in Jesus Christ'.

Faith in ministry

As the school is the specific field of the Brothers' apostolate 'the place where the Brothers spend most of their time during the day' (Meditation 92,3), the Founder is led to establish an important distinction in principle between:

— their personal faith which is the interior inspiration of all their Christian conduct and

— their ministerial faith which, in addition, animates and makes fruitful all their apostolic activity:

Your simple faith in the mysteries may be enough for you yourself, but not enough if you are to be able to give them what they need.[8]

Your faith should be for you a light which guides you in all things, and a shining light for those whom you instruct, to lead them on the way to heaven.[9]

Do you have a faith as lively as that of the saint? You are bound to excel in the Spirit of Faith, for you have to teach the children the maxims of the Holy Gospel and the mysteries of our religion.[10]

Do you have a faith that is such that it is able to touch the hearts of your students and inspire them with a Christian spirit? This is the greatest miracle you could perform and the one God asks of you, for this is the purpose of your work.[11]

There is a Christian viewpoint, a way of seeing and judging that is in harmony with the Gospel, which the Founder calls 'the spirit of Christianity', the 'Christian spirit' or 'the spirit of Jesus Christ' and which he asks the Brothers to develop in the hearts of the pupils since 'the just, that is, true Christians, live by faith'.[12]

The spirit of the Institute is nothing other than this Christian mentality applied to the Brothers' situation in the Institute. In the Church, they are Christians with a specific role, ministers of the Word in the mission field of the school, a situation which necessarily affects their view of the world and of life, as does also their prayer and activity.

The three effects of the spirit of faith

The spirit of faith harmonizes three privileged areas of the Brother's personal life with the Lasallian ideal, three areas in which a Brother must react and express himself insofar as he is a follower of John Baptist de La Salle. Indeed the Brother cannot truly consider himself to be or to be recognized as a member of the Institute, except insofar as the spirit of faith animates and sustains the following three characteristics of his deepest self namely, his judgment, his commitment and his discernment.

Lasallian judgment

The first effect of the spirit of faith is 'not to look upon anything but with the eyes of faith', that is, 'to see created things as God sees them, and as faith requires us to think of them'.[13] The 1987 Rule (article 5) says more soberly, 'It is by faith that the Brothers judge all earthly realities in the light of the Gospel'.

Enlightened in this way, human beings cease to be captivated or allured by creation. They see it rather as a mirror reflecting the action of the Creator. Their interests and affections are directed to God to whom alone they are attached. In this way they can be like 'those who have to deal with the world and who should not become engrossed in it … because the world as we know it is passing away' (1 Corinthians 7:31).

Judgment of this nature becomes the norm for the entire life of the Brother and the motivating force for his day-to-day activity:

> 'Let your first care be to act by the Spirit of faith, and not by caprice, inclination or whim. Do not let yourself be governed by human customs, or those of the world, or by mere reason, but solely by faith and the words of Jesus Christ, making these the rule of your conduct.[14]

The first piece of advice that the Founder gave to Brother Anastase, (28 January 1711) was:

> apply yourself, above all, my very dear Brother, to be motivated by faith, so that your actions may be well done.[15]

The Brother who is influenced by this 'judge then act' process, once he has participated in the knowledge that God has of his own creation, is able to apply the ensuing enlightenment to every aspect of his daily living and so motivate and direct his life in accord with the Gospel.

Lasallian commitment

The second effect of the spirit of faith is 'not to do anything but in view of God' that is, 'to perform all our actions solely to glorify and please God',[16] which article 5 of the 1987 Rule translates, 'by faith, the Brothers, co-operators with Jesus Christ, consecrate their whole existence to the building up of the kingdom of God through the service of education'.

This article of the Rule is concerned, of course, with Lasallian ministry. But it would be an extreme pity if it were to be interpreted as applicable in the daily life of the Brother only to such time as was spent with the young and their formation. The Brother's life is unified and the two divisions he makes of it, one in the school and the other in community, cannot really be separated, because of a constant process of osmosis taking place between the two. The two divisions, working as one, contribute to the realization of the pastoral purpose of the Institute, as if they were a modern re-enactment 'of the words of the Apostles on the occasion of the ordination of deacons 'we shall continue to devote ourselves to prayer and the service of the word' (Acts 6:4).

John Baptist de La Salle, who asked Brother Anastase to 'be motivated by faith' in his actions, also advised Brother Hubert (1 June 1706): 'Always have God in view in what you do; this is important if your actions are to be done in a Christian manner'.[17]

The Founder gives a reason for this as follows:

> since God in the next life is the purpose and goal of all your actions, he should be this also in this life, especially in your state which demands of you a high degree of perfection.[18]

He justifies this demand by recourse to the consecration that the Brother has made of his whole being to the Most Holy Trinity:

> You offered yourself to God when you left the world … you should not be content to have made this offering of yourselves to God once; you should renew this offering everyday and consecrate all your actions to him by not performing any of them except for him.[19]

At this point we can acknowledge the intrinsic harmony that exists between the first two effects of the spirit of faith. The Lasallian manner of judging which has its source in God is complemented by Lasallian commitment, which has God as its ultimate end. God, the alpha and omega, is not only the starting point of our life and activity but also its summit or culmination.

The Brother, with his judgment in conformity with the divine intelligence of creation has, by his commitment, made his will conform to the divine will.

Lasallian discernment

The third effect of the spirit of faith is 'to attribute all to God'.[20] *The Collection* explains it thus: 'It is to accept both good and evil as coming from God's hands'.

Article 5 of the 1987 Rule comments, 'It is by faith that the Brothers are aware of God's presence in their undertakings, their cares and their joys: It is by faith the Brothers learn to see in every happening and in every person, especially in the poor, a sign and a call of the Spirit'.

The area for application for this third effect is then no longer what the Brothers think (as for the first effect) nor what they do (as for the second effect) but what happens to them and what they feel deeply. It is easy to discover in the above texts mention of the three following elements.

— the uncertainties of life (situations which occur, tasks which arise, needs to be attended to, encounters, dangers): 'their undertakings', 'every happening', 'every person', 'the poor';

— a positive or negative reaction to such uncertainties, as shown in feelings, in affectivity: 'good and evil', 'their cares and their joys';

— the manifestation, by means of this double reality, of the presence of God in human lives and of his will for us: 'as coming from God's hands', 'of God's presence', 'sign and call of the Spirit'.

What God reaches in us in this way is not only one of our faculties, our intelligence or will, but the deepest recesses of our being, our very 'heart', to use the word so often employed by John Baptist de La Salle.

By judgment we see only God in his creation: by discernment we discover God in all the events that impact on us. By commitment we will to place all activity at God's disposal, by discernment we are aware of God's total dominion over our entire existence. Judgment and commitment can be seen as reaction and response to the signs and calls that Lasallian discernment makes known.

God, our beginning and our end, is present in the interval between, setting up from end to end across the passing of our days and the variety of our states of mind a creative continuity which gives us identity. It is like a river flowing from its source to its mouth, or like the regulated succession of the letters of the alphabet, with alpha at the beginning and omega at the end.

By means of these three privileged areas where the spirit of faith is at work, God is concerned with the entire warp and woof of the Brothers' life which he directs 'in order to bring salvation to the least and to the poorest'.[21]

Important observations

The harmony of the effects of the spirit of faith is an indication of the universality of God's influence in what constitutes and concerns each one of us. We frequent and bear within ourselves a world filled with God. All that comes to us from the outside (creatures, events), and all that is born in us and from us (conceptions, actions) stem from God 'since it is in him, that we live and move and exist' (Acts 17:28). This is a truth which the concluding words of Chapter 2 of the 1987 Rule on 'Mission' translate as follows:

The entire life of the Brothers is transformed by the presence of the Lord, who calls, consecrates, sends and saves.[22]

It is just as important to emphasize the radical nature of the spirit of faith. This is evident if we examine the repeated use of the expressions of an absolute nature such as 'not to look upon anything', 'not to do anything', 'to attribute all', 'all earthly realities', 'their whole being', 'in every person'. If we re-read Chapter 2 of the original Rule of 1717 we constantly find these expressions and others of like nature, such as 'always', 'not a single day', 'not a single deed'. In no other subject has the founder proved to be so thorough, so dogmatic.

The reason for this emphasis is surely to be found in the all-important need for the followers of John Baptist De La Salle to be possessed of the spirit of faith. It is a question of authenticity, one might even say of life or death. This is the spirit of the Brothers; without it they do not exist. To give more forceful expression to this, the Founder has recourse to particularly severe terms:

> and those who have lost it, should be looked upon as dead members, and they should look upon themselves as such; because they are deprived of the life and grace of their state and they should be convinced that it will be very difficult for them to preserve the grace of God.[23]

The efficacy of the Brothers' ministry and fidelity to their vocation therefore, depend upon a triple priority:

— the purity of vision in their judgments;
— the purity of intention in their commitment;
— the purity of heart in their discernment.

4. Zeal

Characteristics of zeal

The simple faith of ordinary Christians cannot satisfy the demands of the Brothers' ministry. They need a faith which reaches to the innermost depths, a faith which saturates them to the extent that there gush forth at all times words and actions that identify them both as teachers and witnesses: they need a faith of a higher order, a 'spirit of faith'.

De La Salle, in his writings, used the word 'zeal' 196 times, but never made use of the expression 'spirit of zeal' (the one exception being in article

7 of the Collection of things on which the Brothers shall converse in their recreations, where this virtue is linked with other religious values lived in the spirit: 'Those who have been remarkable for the spirit of mortification and of zeal for the salvation of their neighbor'.[24]

Does this one occurrence of the expression 'spirit of zeal' obscure the idea that zeal, being of its nature something highly passion-driven, exists only insofar as it is expressed in individual determinate acts, and that it never itself attains its full dimension except, when by reason of a radical transformation of the soul, it manifests itself in strength and perseverance? Is it not in fact oriented towards the salvation of others? 'The Kingdom of Heaven has been subjected to violence and the violent are taking it by storm' (Matthew 11:12). We need then, in accord with the Founder's thinking, see in the expression 'spirit of zeal' a regrettable redundancy.

The adjective which in his writing he uses most frequently to characterize zeal is 'ardent' (16 times out of 47 examples.) But we also find the use of the words, unwearyingly, certain, generous, intrepid, admirable, surprising, incomparable, far-reaching, extraordinary ... all words which originate in a forceful register, and which, in their use, express the enthusiasm of their author and especially the conviction that zeal can never be confined to mediocrity.

The object of zeal

Indeed zeal is a passion which John Baptist de La Salle defined 'as the opposite of envy', that other passion 'which leads us to be displeased with the goods and success to which our neighbor attains and the satisfaction we take in the misfortune he experiences'.[25]

Zeal with regard to students

Among all the goods the Brothers could wish to obtain for their pupils (their neighbours by choice) zeal would have them aim for the best, 'the one thing necessary' (Luke 10:42), namely their students' earthly and eternal salvation:

> It is your duty in your state to combine a life of seclusion and mortification with zeal for your neighbour's salvation, because the purpose of your work is to labor continually for the Christian education of children. Apply yourself to this work with all possible care, for if you do you will not be able to count how many you have gained for God and made true Christians.[26]

> Have you up to the present looked upon the salvation of your students as

your personal responsibility during the whole time they are under your guidance? You have exercises which are arranged for your own sanctification, but if you have an ardent zeal for the salvation of those whom you are called to instruct, you will not fail to perform them and to relate them to this intention. In doing this you will draw on your students the graces needed to contribute to their salvation, and you can be assured that if you act this way for their salvation, God himself will take responsibility for yours.[27]

Zeal with regard to the Church

This apostolate contributes in a very efficacious way to the building up of the Church:

> You must also show the Church what love you have for her and give her proof of your zeal, since it is for the Church (which is the body of Jesus Christ) that you work. You have become her ministers according to the order God has given you to dispense his word. Since the Church has a great zeal for the sanctification of her children, it is your duty to share in her zeal, so that you can say to God as the holy King David: 'the zeal of your house has consumed me'. For this house is none other than the church, since the faithful form this building which has been built on the foundation of the Apostles and raised up by Jesus Christ, who is the main cornerstone.[28]

Zeal as regards God himself

Zeal also has as its ultimate end of glory of God:

> These are the kinds of maxims and practices you must continually inspire in your disciples if you have any zeal for their salvation. This will be the way you will show yourselves zealous for the glory of God; since these maxims can come only from God (being contrary to human inclination), it is a work of zeal for the honor and glory to God to inspire children to put them into practice.[29]

> God will bless all you do with zeal for love of him.[30]

Zeal: understanding what it means

Completely directed towards the realization of the purpose of the Institute, zeal projects on this purpose a definitive light, confirming if there was still need for it that the Brothers' purpose is not the act of teaching. The Brothers' consecration, their entire way of life, has no other objective than the evangelization of the young and the supernatural fruits that should ensue—namely, to use the very words of the Founder, their 'conversion' and 'their sanctification': 'Ask [God] for the grace, needed to procure the conversion of their hearts'[31]

> Compare your zeal for the sanctification of your disciples with that of this great saint, for you should spend your entire life trying to make them good Christians.[32]

Teaching is but one means. The Brothers who through obedience, engage in other occupations know quite well that these occupations have meaning and value only within the frame of the pastoral ministry of the Institute: they do not confuse their employment with the purpose and end of that employment.

The practice of zeal

Moreover, however privileged teaching may be and across all the forms it takes today to respond to the present needs of the young, it does not exhaust zeal's field of application, the space where it is exercised. To cover this area, the 1718 rule goes into detail:

> The Brothers of the Society shall strive by prayer, instruction, and by their vigilance and good conduct in school to procure the salvation of the children confided to their care, bringing them up in piety and in a truly Christian spirit, that is, according to the rules and maxims of the Gospel.[33]

Prayer

The word 'prayer' in the above citation shows that it is indispensable for the Brothers. Lasallian zeal is expressed, first of all, by the act of prayer, but not just any kind of prayer. As we have already seen in regard to faith, the simple prayer of a Christian cannot be adequate for the Brothers whose apostolic commitment requires from them a life of ministerial prayer on which the Founder insisted in a special way. It had to involve, as it were, a double movement. The Brother prays first of all for himself, that God may give him the light to be passed on to the children and for the graces that he needs with the help of the Holy Spirit to effect a fruitful proclamation of the Gospel message. Next the Brother prays for his students that they might receive his 'instructions' with a well-disposed heart and that they try to implement them in their daily lives. In this way the finality of the Institute is attained.

This development of Lasallian prayer is to be found in an oft-quoted text from the sixth *Meditation for the Time of Retreat* (MTR 198,1), where the symbol of Jacob's ladder is exploited. The same development, with a dramatic emphasis unusual for De La Salle and so more significant of his interest in the subject, occurs in the last two points of Meditation No.37, i.e. the parable of the importunate friend (Luke 11:5-8) is being examined. Each of these two points is devoted to one of the two phases of the prayer:

> 1.God sends them to you so that you may give them the spirit of Christianity and educate them according to the maxims of the Gospel ... Ask God, then, for what you lack and to give you what you need in full measure, namely, the Christian spirit and deep religious convictions ... their ignorance is great, their need is pressing, and you have nothing to satisfy their needs ... Will you then abandon them and leave them without any instruction? Have recourse to God, knock on the door, pray, beg him insistently and even importunately. The three loaves which you should ask for represent knowledge of the three Divine Persons. If you obtain this from God, you will have what will satisfy those who come to you in their need for instruction (*Meditations*, 37,2).

> 2.This God of goodness places them in your hands and undertakes to give them everything you ask of him for them: piety, self-control, reserve, purity, the avoidance of companions who could be dangerous to them ... He wants you to ask him for those blessings for them, frequently, fervently and insistently. In this way, thanks to your care, nothing will be lacking to them that they need for their salvation (*Meditations*, 37,3).

Instruction

The word 'instruction' as it is normally used in John Baptist de La Salle's writings has a religious significance and indicates what he also called 'catechisms'. We find, however, in the fourteenth *Meditation for the Time of Retreat*:

> 'You will have to give an account to God ... whether you have not preferred to teach secular subjects, such as reading, writing, arithmetic ... to those which are of much greater importance because they contribute to the support of religion, though you ought not neglect the former, since they are strictly required of you' (*MTR*, 206,1).

We know that the Founder, even if he gives religion pride of place among all the different subjects taught at school, treats them all with the utmost care, since such care ensures that all, in their separate ways, play their part in the complete and harmonious formation of the future adult Christian.

These 'instructions' take up again those of God, of Christ, of the Apostles, which the Holy Scriptures pass on, those which the Church addresses unceasingly, to the faithful and to all humankind through the voices of its ministers, doctors and saints. And each evening before leaving school, the children recite the following prayer:

> My God I thank you for all the instructions that you have given me today in school. Grant me the grace to draw profit from them and to be faithful in putting them into practice.[34]

The fruitful results arising from instructions are, for John Baptist de La Salle, the measure of their worth and significance. He points out their major effect:

> This means that you are called to lay the foundation for the building of the Church when you instruct children in the mystery of the most Holy Trinity and the mysteries accomplished by Jesus Christ when he was on earth. For according to saint Paul, without faith it is impossible to please God and consequently be saved and enter the homeland of heaven, because faith is the foundation of the hope that we have. The knowledge, then, that each must have of the faith, the instruction that must be given concerning the faith to those who are ignorant of it, is one of the most important things in our religion.[35]

Still one essential condition remains for the Brother to fulfil:

> Since you are ambassadors and ministers of Jesus Christ in the work that you do, you must act as representing Jesus Christ himself. He wants your disciples to see him in you and receive your instructions as if he were giving them to them. They must be convinced that your instructions are the truth of Jesus Christ who speaks with your mouth, that it is only in his name that you teach, and that it is he who has given you authority over them.[36]

This postulates a condition which requires a corresponding attitude among the pupils.

> 'They will have received the word of God in your catechism lessons not as the word of men but as the word of God which is powerfully at work in them'.[37]

Thus zeal is linked with and espouses the spirit of faith. Ought we be surprised that this is so?

Vigilance

Vigilance, one of the twelve virtues of a good teacher, has its origin in God.

Since parents who are poor and unable in fact to assume their responsibilities as educators,

> it is characteristic of the providence of God, and of his vigilance over human conduct to substitute for fathers and mothers persons who have enough knowledge and zeal to bring children to the knowledge of God and of his mysteries.[38]

But this virtue is required of the Brother first of all in his dealings with 'people of the world' in order not to 'to adopt their spirit'; the virtue is needed in Community, if he is to edify his confreres; and especially in regard to himself, as the Founder recommended to Gabriel Drolin in Rome.

> I know, too, that there is a great deal of corruption where you are and that you have to be very careful and watchful [vigilant] over yourself not to get caught up in it. Blessed be God that he has given you the grace to keep from it up till now.[39]

A similar general piece of advice is to be found expressed more positively in the following quotation from one of the Founder's meditations:

> What great vigilance religious should exercise over all their conduct so that their actions may be such as they ought to be in order to please God.[40]

The Conduct of Schools devotes an entire chapter to the 'vigilance of the teacher' which appears at the head of the 'nine principal things which can contribute to establishing and maintaining order in schools'.[41]

Vigilance is without doubt a matter of 'supervising'—'The vigilance of teachers in school consists particularly of three things: correcting all the words which are mispronounced by a student when reading; making all of the students who have the same lesson follow along when any one of them is reciting; and enforcing a very strict silence'[42]—but more importantly of 'watching over' with concern. In the Christian school, traditional school practices take on an absolutely new meaning. This is so because the Christian teacher acts in view of the greatest good for the students, as is explained by the final part of the text we quoted at the beginning:

> You, then, whom God has called to this Ministry, work according to the grace that has been given to you to instruct by teaching, and to exhort by encouraging those who are entrusted to your care, guiding them with attention and vigilance, in order to fulfill toward them the principal duty of fathers and mothers toward their children.[43]

Correction

The text quoted above from the 1718 Rule does not single out correction, which really belongs as part of vigilance, of which it is an essential consequence. De La Salle devotes the eighth chapter of his Rule, as well as the fifth chapter of the second part of *The Conduct of Christian Schools*, to correction. This is enough to emphasize the importance he attaches to the matter. Elsewhere the Founder treats it in quite a new way, a way which must be qualified as pastoral. He sees within the heart of each fault committed at school the sin which is at its source, whether it be laziness, disobedience, anger or pride, and his aim is, by means of correction, to provide a remedy. To correct, then, is no longer to punish an offender for a misdemeanour, but rather to put the culprit back on the right path, that of good order.

It is worth while noting that with the Founder the word Correction is often written with a capital, as if beyond the need for discipline, and in addition to the proper functioning of the school. Thanks to the strict respect for regulations, the major reality in view is God's order, the order that presided at creation and which God willed for the affairs of humanity. This viewpoint, stemming from faith and zeal, explains the conditions that the Founder says should accompany the act of correction both on the part of the teacher and that of the student. Thus we read:

> [Correction] must be pure and disinterested. That is to say correction must be administered purely for the glory of God and for the fulfillment of God's holy will …
>
> Second, correction must be charitable i.e. administered out of a motive of true charity toward the student who receives it, and for the salvation of the student's soul …
>
> Third, correction must be just … Fourth … proper and suitable to the fault for which it is administered. That is to say, it must be proportionate … Fifth, correction must be moderate. That is to say, it should be rather less rigorous than more rigorous.
>
> Sixth, correction must be peaceable. Those who administer it should not be moved to anger. Those to whom it is administered should receive it in a peaceable manner and with tranquillity of mind and outward restraint. Seventh, it must be prudent on the part of the teacher. Eighth, it must be willingly accepted by the students. Ninth, those punished should be respectful. They should receive punishment with submission and respect, as they would receive a chastisement with which God would punish them. Tenth, it must be silent. In the first place, the teacher must be silent and

should not speak. In the second place the student must be silent and ought not to say a single word, cry out or make any noise whatsoever.[44]

These precepts illustrate, in concrete fashion, the fundamental principle in the Founder's educational thinking: 'the necessity of joining gentleness to firmness in the guidance of children'.[45] We need to re-read all these pages to discover therein the pastor who did not fear to ask his Brothers,

> Do you have these sentiments of charity and tenderness toward the poor children whom you have to educate? Do you take advantage of their affection for you to lead them to God? If you have for them the firmness of a father to restrain and withdraw them from misbehavior, you must also have for them the tenderness of a mother to draw them to you, and to do for them all the good that depends on you.[46]

Good example

We know already how Lasallian catechists find themselves obliged to take into account the bond that exists between the excellence and strictness of the doctrine they teach and of the example of their manner of living. Because they are believers, they have chosen to consecrate their lives to passing on their faith and the least of their deeds and gestures bear witness to this complete fidelity to the God whom they proclaim. In the presence of their students, they can make their own the words of St Paul: 'Take me for your model, as I take Christ' (1 Corinthians 11:1).

But if they lived their faith only at school, they would be acting the hypocrite. In all aspects of their lives their mission demands that they be truly Christian. John Baptist de La Salle expresses this in radical fashion when he writes:

> Because in your state of life you are called to procure the sanctification of your pupils, you should be holy yourself in no ordinary degree, for you must communicate this holiness to them both by your good example and by the words of salvation which you must address to them every day.[47]

The purpose of the Lasallian school is the sanctification of the students by means of the totality of the formation they receive, even if a more specialized role is assigned to the study of religion and to an apprenticeship in 'the virtues and maxims of the Gospel' and to the acquisition and development in the students of the 'Spirit of Christianity'. As for the finality of the Institute, this is no less than the sanctification of the Brothers by the exercise of their apostolic ministry in accord with the 'spirit of their state'.

The fullness of zeal

Just as faith grows to its proper fullness, so also zeal aspires to its complete realization. Zeal, unlike any other passion, can lead to extremes in three ways: it can lead to crime, to madness and death. The Founder was spared from the effects of the first, when crime arises from a zeal that has become fanaticism. The two other excesses are to be found both in his life and in his writings.

How many times, at the outset of his work, do we find his contemporaries, shocked by a conversion they did not understand, accusing him of losing his wits, of having 'lost his mind?'[48] He justified his actions later by reference to saint Paul:

> God changed the wisdom of the world into folly. [St Paul], enlightened by God's wisdom and inspiration, says that the world did not recognize God through its wisdom, so it pleased God through the folly of the preaching of the Gospel to save those who accept the faith.[49]

How many times do we find among his first companions certain individuals who died very young after only a few years of walking with him, prematurely worn out by the fatigue of their employment and the excessive ascetical practices of the Community? The Founder motivated their conduct with expressions like the following:

> Let it be clear then, in all your conduct towards the children who are entrusted to you, that you look upon yourselves as ministers of God carrying out your Ministry with love and a sincere and true zeal, accepting with much patience the difficulties you have to suffer, willing to be despised by men and to be persecuted, even to give your life for Jesus in the fulfillment of your ministry.[50]

> You must in imitation of the great Apostle encourage them to live in a manner worthy of God, since he has called them to his kingdom and his glory; your zeal must go so far in this that in order to achieve it, you are ready to give your very life, so dear to you are the children.[51]

After the Last Supper, Jesus said to his apostles, 'You can have no greater love than to lay down your life for your his friends' (John 15:13).

Lasallian Texts

A Lasallian vocabulary for faith

1. Faith

To believe something is to know it only on the word of another and to give assent to it. There are two kinds of faith, divine faith and human faith (*CL*, 20, 2; *Duties of a Christian*, 1, p. 101, 2, 3).

2. The truth of faith

Any matter proposed for the faith of Christians in the area of dogma and morals:
We must not be satisfied with making acts of faith on speculative matters only, that is to say on truths that we cannot but believe; we must also make acts of practical faith that is to say on truths that are to be put into practice (*CL*, 20, 6, *Duties of a Christian*, 1, p. 101, 2 , 3).

3. The maxims of faith

A passage of Holy Scripture that expresses a truth of faith:
In order to bring the children whom you instruct to take on the Christian spirit, you must teach them the practical truths of faith in Jesus Christ and the maxims of the Holy Gospel with at least as much care as you teach the truths that are purely doctrinal *(MTR*, 194, 3).
Truths and maxims are formulas of the faith.

4. The motive of faith

An article of faith determining an action and inspiring it.

5. The view of faith

The interpretation proposed for an action in order to relate it to God.
Motives and views of faith are isolated acts of faith.

6. 'The eyes of faith', 'the light of faith'

The disposition, more or less latent, of the practical judgment, a way of acting based on faith and having recourse to motives and views of faith.

7. The sentiment of faith

A spiritual movement of the soul, or within the soul, the animating force of the Christian life and of the Brother's apostolic activity.

8. The fullness of faith

The ultimate degree of faith according to each person's capacity:

Each of you must judge himself soberly by the standard of faith God has given him (Romans, 12:3).

… according to the fullness which you have destined for me', *(Encountering God in the Mind and Heart,* p.55).

… with all the fullness of which through the mercy and grace of God I am capable of receiving' *(CL*, 14, 92, *EM*, 10, 244; *Encountering God*, pp.292, 244a).

… he wanted to share the fullness of his faith with those of his nation' *(Meditations*, 87, 2).

Lasallian texts relative to the spirit of faith

1. Basic Text

Chapter II of the Rule of 1718.
— *CL*, 25, 18, 19, 20.
— Rule (1987), pp. 15, 16, 17.

2. For an authentic reading of Saint John Baptist de La Salle

— Collection of various Short Treatises, pp.30 – 38.
— From the general chapter of 1986.
— Rule of 1987, articles 5, 6, 7, 8, pp. 24, 25, 26.

3. Supplementary texts

— Letter of 28 January 1711 to Brother Anastase (No. 72, p. 191).
— Faith, Obedience, Regularity.
— Collection of various Short Treatises, pp. 66, 67, 68, 69.

Concerning the spirit of the Institute

That which is of the utmost importance, and to which the greatest attention should be given in an Institute is that all who compose it possess the spirit peculiar to it; that the novices apply themselves to acquire it; and that those who are already members make it their first care to preserve and increase it in themselves; for it is this spirit that should animate all their actions, be the motive of their whole conduct, and those who do not possess it and those who have lost it, should be looked upon as dead members, and they should look upon themselves as such; because they are deprived of the life and grace of their state; and they should be convinced that it will be very difficult for them to preserve the grace of God.

The spirit of this Institute is, first, a spirit of faith, which should induce those who compose it not to look upon anything but with the eyes of faith, not to do anything but in view of God, and to attribute all to God, always entering into these sentiments of Job. 'The Lord gave and the Lord has taken away, as it has pleased the Lord, so it be done', and into other similar sentiments so often expressed in Holy Scripture and uttered by the Patriarchs of old.

In order to enter into this spirit and live up to it:

1. The Brothers of this Society shall have a most profound respect for the Holy Scriptures; and, in proof thereof, they shall always carry the New Testament about them, and pass no day without reading some of it, through a sentiment of faith, respect and veneration for the divine words contained therein, looking upon it as their first and principal rule.

2. The Brothers of this Society shall animate all their actions with sentiments of faith; and, in performing them, they shall always have in view the orders and the will of God, which they shall adore in all things, and by which they shall be careful to regulate their conduct.

For this purpose they shall apply themselves to have great control over their senses and to use them only through necessity, not wishing to use them but according to the order and the will of God.

They shall make it heir study to exercise continual watchfulness over themselves, so as not to perform, if possible, a single action from natural impulse, through custom or any human movement; but they shall act so as to perform them all by the guidance of God, through the movement of His Spirit, and with the intention of pleasing Him.

They shall pay as much attention as they can to the holy presence of God, and take care to renew it from time to time; being well convinced that they should think only of Him and of what He ordains, that is, what concerns their duty and employment.

They shall banish from their minds all vain ideas and thoughts that might withdraw them from these practices, which are very important for them, and without which they can neither acquire nor preserve the spirit of their state.

Secondly, the spirit of their Institute consists in an ardent zeal for the instruction of children, and for bringing them up in the fear of God, inducing them to preserve their innocence if they have not lost it, and inspiring them with a great aversion and horror for sin and whatever might cause them to lose purity.

In order to enter this spirit, the Brothers of the Society shall strive by prayer, instruction, and by their vigilance and good conduct in school, to procure the salvation of the children confided to their care, bringing them up in piety and in a truly Christian spirit, that is, according to the rules and maxims of the Gospel.

(Chapter 2: Common Rules , 1718)

Letter to Brother Anastase, 28 January 1711

(*Letters*, No. 72, p. 191)

Apply yourself above all, my dear Brother, to be motivated by faith so that your actions may be well done.

I am very glad that your whole aim and intention is to do God's will.

In order to succeed in this you should strive particularly to be entirely submissive and to observe your rules well, for it is in this way especially that you will carry out God's will.

Take great care about prayer and try to do all your actions in a prayerful spirit. The more faithful you are in these matters, the more God will bless you.

Often recollect yourself in order to renew and strengthen in your mind the remembrance of the presence of God.

The more you try to achieve this the easier you will find it to perform your actions and carry out your duties well.

I ask God to give you in abundance the spirit of your state and
I am, my very dear Brother,
Devotedly yours in Our Lord
De La Salle

Letter of 28 January 1711

To Brother Anastase
(Letters, No. 72, p. 191)

Apply yourself above all my very dear Brother to be motivated by faith so that your actions may be well done.

I am very glad that your whole aim and intention is to do God's will.

Common Rule, 1718

Chapter 2 (CL 25) and Rule, 1987 ed. pp. 15, 16, 17)

The Brothers of this Society shall animate all their actions with sentiments of faith.

And in performing them they shall always have in view the orders and the will of God.

In order to succeed in this you should strive particularly to be entirely submissive and to observe your rules well.

often recollect yourself ...

in order to renew and strengthen in your mind the remembrance of the presence of God.

The more you try to achieve this ...

the easier you will find it to perform your actions and carry out your duties well.

I ask God to give you in abundance the spirit of your state

Which [will] they shall adore in all things and by which they shall be careful to regulate their conduct.

They shall make it their study to exercise continual watchfulness over themselves.

They shall pay as much attention as they can to the holy presence of God.

And take care to renew it from time to time ...

being well convinced that they should think only of Him and of what he ordained i.e. of what concerns their duty and employment.

They shall banish from their minds all vain ideas and thoughts that might withdraw them from these practices which are very important to them, and without which they can neither acquire or preserve the spirit of their state.

Between the first three points of the letter and those that follow there is inserted a paragraph on the spirit of prayer, and in chapter two of the Rule we find included, after the third point, a paragraph on the control of the senses.

Our prayer as part of ministry

The spirit of the Brothers' state

1. In all we do for the glory of God and the salvation of souls, we should undertake nothing without praying to ask God for the light and grace we need to succeed in whatever we undertake for him in this holy ministry, which can succeed only insofar as we are aided by his help and directed by his Holy Spirit (Meditations, 107,1).

2. Let all your time, following the example of Saint Martin, be spent in these two things: asking God insistently for the salvation of those who are under your guidance, and seeking and helping them use these means (Meditations, 189,3).

3. Be assured that the more you devote yourself to prayer, the more you will also do well in your work. For, since of yourself you are not able to do anything well for the salvation of souls, you should often turn to God to obtain from him what your profession obliges you to give to others. For it is God, says Saint James, who is the father of lights and it is from him that every perfect gift comes down. This includes everything that is given and is needed to procure our salvation. Earnestly beg of God this spirit of prayer *(Meditations*, 95,1).

4. Often reflect that you should be a man of prayer, because you must pray not only for yourself but also for those whom you have to guide and for the needs of their soul (*Meditations*, 187,2).

5. You must then devote yourself very much to prayer in order to succeed in your ministry. You must constantly represent the needs of your disciples to Jesus Christ, explaining to him the difficulties you have experienced in guiding them. Jesus Christ, seeing that you regard him as the one who can do everything in your work and yourself as an instrument that ought to be moved only by him, will not fail to grant you what you ask of him (*MTR* ,196, 1).

6. Have you up to the present looked upon the salvation of your students as your personal responsibility during the whole time they are under your guidance? You have exercises which are arranged for your own sanctification, but if you have an ardent zeal for the salvation of those whom you are called to instruct you will not fail to perform them and relate them to this intention. In doing this you will draw on your students the graces needed to contribute to their salvation, and you can be assured that if you act in this way for their salvation, God himself will take responsibility for yours (*MTR*, 205, 2).

Prayer as part of ministry

The fruit of instructions

7. Since you are the ambassadors and ministers of Jesus Christ in the work that you do, you must act as representing Jesus Christ himself. He wants your disciples to see him in you and receive your instructions as if he were giving them to them. They must be convinced that your instructions are the truth of Jesus Christ who speaks with your mouth, that it is only in his name that you teach, and that it is he who has given you authority over them … In order for you to fulfill this duty with as much perfection and exactness as God requires of you, frequently give yourselves to the Spirit of our Lord to act in your work only under his influence, so that your own spirit may have no part in it. This Holy Spirit then will come upon them generously so that they will be able to possess fully the Christian Spirit (*MTR* 195,2).

8. This is why you must ask him earnestly that all your instructions be given life by his Spirit and draw all their power from him. Just as he is the one who enlightens everyone coming into the world, he is also the one who enlightens the minds of your students and leads them to love and to practice the good that you teach them (*MTR*, 195,3).

9. The duty you have of obtaining grace not only for yourselves but also for others and of learning how to touch hearts should make you apply yourselves very specially to prayer, for this is the exercise designed for you by God to procure his graces (*Meditations*, 129,2).

10. Your work will be of little value if you do not have for your purpose the salvation of souls ... The more ardently you apply yourselves to prayer for the good of the souls entrusted to you, the more God will help you find the skill to touch their hearts (*Meditations*, 148, 2).

11. You have the advantage of sharing in the duties of the apostles by teaching catechism daily to the children under your guidance and by instructing them in the maxims of the Holy Gospel; you will not do them much good, however, if you do not possess in full measure the spirit of prayer, which gives a holy fervor to your words and makes them able to penetrate very effectively the depths of the hearts of your students (*Meditations*, 159, 2).

12. In your work you do not have to war against heretics, but against the immature inclinations of children that urge them strongly to evil. You will not overcome these by merely natural learning, but by the Spirit of God and the fullness of his grace and you will not draw this grace upon yourself except by the power of prayer (*Meditations*, 161, 2).

13. The obligation that you have to instruct children and bring them up in a spirit of Christianity should make you very assiduous in prayer, in order to obtain from God the graces you need to carry out your work well and to draw upon yourselves the light you must have to know how to form Jesus Christ in the hearts of the children who are entrusted to your guidance, and give them the Spirit of God. Realize that to fill yourselves with God as much as you should in the state in which Providence has placed you, you are obliged to converse frequently with God (*Meditations*, 80,2).

Chapter 9

'Whether to be the Father or not?'

1. The grain of mustard seed (Matthew 13:31-32)

'... in that country'

In 1707, at Rouen, John Baptist de La Salle came to an agreement with the members of the Poorhouse Board that, in exchange for a miserably poor stipend, he would make available ten Brothers for the city's schools. He found lodgings for them outside the General Hospital in a house altogether too small for their number and under conditions of extreme poverty. Also in 1707, in Paris, he met for the first time, in February or March, the young Jean-Charles Clement who was to play a dramatic role in his life.

In the course of the same year, he was especially engaged in strengthening and extending the expansion of the Institute south of the Loire, beyond that pseudo- frontier which marked the limit of what was then generally called the North of France. The movement had begun in 1703 with the opening of a school in Avignon, in Papal territory. He had continued on to Marseilles in 1706, then to Mende, Valréas, Alès, Grenoble. Each year saw new births.

In thus answering in positive fashion the requests made by bishops, priests and pious persons, the Founder was not simply following his own desire, legitimate though it was, to develop the work to which he had consecrated himself and which he believed was not his but God's. He sought only the good of the Church, which, following the Council of Trent, was striving to renew its evangelising mission. His intention was that the Society of the

Christian Schools would become an especially fruitful instrument of such regeneration.

This is why he included a universal ambition in his pastoral zeal, as these extracts from the letters to Brother Gabriel Drolin testify: 'We have Brothers in Marseilles where they began a short time ago. They have 200 students and that in one school only. There are schools in four parts of the town, all of which the Brothers will eventually have'.[1] 'Since the Pope has six schools in Rome, it would be very desirable if they were in the hands of our Brothers ... We have just opened schools at Versailles, Boulogne-sur-Mer and Moulins. Pray that God may increase them more and more.'[2]

A new service for the Institute

The first result of this expansion in the south was the necessity De La Salle now felt of sharing with other Brothers a responsibility which until then he had carried alone: the visitation of the communities and the schools.

Being kept in Paris and then at Rouen, he had since 1703 entrusted a very wide mandate to Brother Ponce, whom he had sent to Darnétal to study the possibility of its being reopened. We read in a letter addressed to Brother Mathias on 30 December 1707: 'Instead of telling your problems to people outside the community, tell them to Brother Ponce or write to him if he is not at Mende. I have delegated him to attend to all that needs to be done for the welfare of the Brothers in that area'.[3]

Only once does De La Salle use the term 'Visitor', in article 11 of Chapter 5 of the Rule of 1718: 'The Brother Director shall not be publicly advertised of his defects unless the Brother Superior of the Institute or the Brother Visitor be present at the time of the Visit'.[4] The Rule of the Brother Director, also from 1718, makes no mention of the Brother Director being dependent, in the exercise of his office, upon anyone other than the Brother Superior. But the extract from Letter 44 (57) already cited gives us a completely correct impression of the role of the Brother Visitor .

Residing in one of the houses of the region, freed from all functions of a professional nature, the Visitor could go to those places where a new foundation was being asked for, examine the conditions of the future establishment (buildings, stipends, social context ...), evaluate the religious needs of the parishes and sound out the motivation of benefactors. Then he could forward his dossier to the Founder for decision. As to the scope of his mission, it consisted in visits to the schools and communities, which, as we know well, work properly only in mutual relationship. Without doubt he would see to it that the former 'went well', that is to say that they realised to the best of their ability the pastoral purpose of Christian education. But he was to devote his most constant care to the Brothers. These continued to write to the Founder each month as had been determined in 1691. But in addition, and on the spot, they would enjoy assistance attentive to all the needs of their life from one invested with the adequate authority to meet them. Taking into account the distance from Paris and the postal delays of the time, this necessary presence would be particularly appreciated: it strengthened the cohesion of the Institute by assuring each one of its members fraternal and effective help.

John Baptist de La Salle saw another advantage in this innovation. For a long time he had wanted the Brothers themselves to take responsibility for the management of the Institute. Twice he had tried to have another Superior elected in his place, but without effect. He took the opportunity to establish an intermediary, a real link for the strengthening of the Institute, whose responsibilities would encompass the good of the Church and that of each Brother.

This measure seemed to him so suitable that he did not hesitate to generalise it. In 1708, he delegated Brother Joseph from Rouen 'to visit the houses of Rethel, Guise, Laon and Rheims'. He renewed Brother Joseph's obedience the following year, adding to it the community of Troyes. Finally, in 1711, he extended his charge to all 'the North'.

An extra-school catechesis

In the meditation which he composed for the Feast of Saint Louis (the most probable period for the composition of the Meditations for Sundays and Feasts would be his stay at Vaugirard from 1692 to 1698), the Founder writes:

> In your work you should unite zeal for the good of the Church with zeal for the good of the state of which your disciples are beginning to be, and one day should be, perfect members. You will procure the good of the Church by making them true Christians and docile to the truths of faith and the maxims of the holy Gospel. You will procure the good of the state by teaching them how to read and write and everything else that pertains to your ministry with regard to exterior things. But piety should be joined to exterior things, otherwise your work would be of little use.[5]

This important text distinguishes sharply how the Brother renders 'to

Caesar that which is Caesar's and to God that which is God's' (Matthew 22:21). At the same time, it affirms once more that, for John Baptist de La Salle, the teaching of what we call profane matters (which he here names 'exterior') belongs just as much to the 'ministry' as does religious education proper: human culture under all its forms is not indifferent to the winning of salvation and there exists no better way of preparing good citizens 'than by making them true Christians'.

This primary intuition establishes the practice, constantly maintained in the Institute, that it should be the same Brother who, after having taught during the day his various lessons, now proposes to his pupils, in the last half-hour before the end of class, his 'instructions ' on 'the mysteries and doctrines of our religion, and the practical maxims which are spread throughout the holy Gospel'.[6] This practice by itself sufficed to exclude any dichotomy in the formation given to the children.

This principle and its application in daily life were to face a serious challenge at Alès, and in 1707, as in the neighbouring township of Vans in 1711.

Let us read once again what Georges Rigault writes on this issue in Volume 1 of his *Histoire Générale de l'Institut* [7]

> The region had for a century now been a Huguenot stronghold. Neither wars nor persecution had succeeded in suppressing heresy on the slopes of the Cevennes and the banks of the Gardon. After the Revocation of the Edict of Nantes and the enforced 'dragonnades', the spirit of the wars of religion had reawakened. Religious assemblies took place in 'the Desert', in gorges and caverns … In 1694 the King obtained from Pope Innocent XII that Alès be erected into a bishopric by detaching it from the diocese of Nîmes. He wanted an ecclesiastical head to be placed in the very midst of hostile crowds in order to rally the Catholic flock, to impose on the Protestants an authority for which the civil power would take responsibility, if needed, to reinforce in its own way. The bishop was François-Maurice Chevalier de Saulx, whose action Blain thus describes:
> 'He called upon Royal authority to oblige fathers and mothers under pain of fines to send their children to the catechism lesson taught by the Brothers on Sundays and feasts … He never tolerated any other schoolmasters but the Brothers; if anyone else, Catholic or heretic, ventured to teach children in secret, he was put into prison'.[8] And Blain goes on to make this comment: 'In this way the Christian schools were filled with students but … the children brought with them the spirit of their parents, spirit and heart in revolt against the instructions they were obliged to listen to'.[9]

The Brothers who, from their very beginning in Rheims, had put up with the insults and ridicule of the mob, who, at Rouen, had had to endure 'sustained contempt and frequent insults ... mud, stones, blows ...'[10] now encountered looks of hatred, stony faces, and consciences which rejected them ... The Brothers, without wavering, continued their apostolate.

John Baptist de La Salle was always inflexible when it was question of the community nature of his Society, as Rigault reminds us:

> ... the failures of his predecessors, the disasters which were the inevitable result of making exceptions and of any deviations in this matter strengthened and justified his intransigence: the Brothers were to be accepted as they were or else they were not available ... He was resigned to be being regarded as 'obstinate, as one who was extremely wedded to his own views'. He preferred to close schools rather than authorise his followers to become choir masters or parish beadles.[11]

However, in the exercise of his pastoral commitment, he gave proof of conspicuous adaptability. After the foundation of a gratuitous Christian school for the poor, he would accept into it children from families in easy circumstances, as at Charonne, for the middle class of Rouen he even established a boarding-school, which necessarily had to charge fees. After having insisted in the Rule that 'they shall neither receive nor keep any pupil in school, unless he attends Catechism',[12] he wrote in the *Conduct of the Christian Schools* that 'by externs are meant those who do not come to the Christian schools during the school week'. Such exceptions existed because a sovereign reason determined them: the service of the Church.[13]

What, according to Blain, was the very source of his vocation, what remained the constant rule of his life, underlay the supreme liberty of which he availed himself in respect of the basic structural principles of his school. His liberty in its turn established that of the Institute which, in the long course of its history, has never ceased to make accommodations often quite revolutionary, in order to adapt itself as well as possible 'to giving a human and Christian education to the young, especially the poor, according to the ministry which the Church has entrusted to it.'[14]

And the cockle ...

Jean-Charles Clement

In 1707, Jean-Charles Clement was a young cleric close to 23 years of age.

De La Salle in glory.
Stained glass, Oakhill Chapel.

Icon of De La Salle by Michael Galovic.

Wood bas relief by Leopoldine Mimovich.

Portrait by Eric Nilan, presented to his old school, De La Salle College, Malvern, to commemorate the 300 years since the birth of John Baptist de La Salle in 1651.

De La Salle with a girl and boy. Bas-relief of E. Piccolruaz
in the foyer of Holy Spirit College, Lakemba,
a co-educational school.

He had seen the school of the rue Princesse in operation and had developed a deep admiration for the Brothers. He attempted to interest John Baptist De La Salle in a scheme of his own for the education of boys. The Founder, who was not willing to move beyond the framework of the Institute, sent him a memorandum in which he set out his own aims and objectives. Jean-Charles then made an offer to revive the Seminary for Country Schoolmasters and, when in 1708 the Brothers opened a school at St Denis, he contemplated purchasing an adjacent house. Because he had not yet reached the age of 25 he did not have the legal capacity to do so, nor did he have as yet sufficient funds at his disposal. It was only after much insisting and promising reimbursement that he succeeded in having the Founder himself make an advance of the necessary outlay. However, because John Baptist was still under the interdiction pronounced by Le Chatelet in 1704, he had no other resources than to have the purchase deed signed by one of his friends, Louis Rogier (not to be confused with Guillaume Rogier, the ecclesiastical superior of the Sisters of the Child Jesus at Rheims, one of those to whom Madame de Maillefer had written thirty years earlier recommending Adrien Nyel).

In the spring of 1709 the Seminary welcomed its first three students. At the end of the same year, Jean-Charles Clement succeeded Mgr de Merinville as Abbot *in commendam*[15] of St Calais some 45 kilometres from Mans. He became archpriest of St Calais and Canon of Le Mans. His feudal rights of revenue extended to four priories and nineteen parishes of the diocese of Le Mans and two priories and five parishes of the diocese of Chartres. He was now rich and had attained his majority.

Discovery of the Midi

The number of schools continued to spread: in 1709 to Macon (which lasted only two years), then, in 1710, to Versailles, Boulogne-sur-Mer and Moulins; then, in 1711, to Les Vans. In this little town near to Alès, in the strongly Protestant sector, the situation took on an impassioned and brutal aspect. The inhabitants "turned to violence. Several times they made attempts on the Brothers' lives. They laid snares for them and set up barricades in the streets to prevent them leaving the house … They gathered as a mob one evening and surrounded the house with the intention of destroying it and massacring the Brothers who lived there. At first they threw stones at the door and through the windows. Later they tried to scale the walls.'[16]

De La Salle declared 'that he was overjoyed to learn that his disciples had been found worthy to suffer humiliations for the honour of their holy religion'.[17]

Though fully confident of the manner in which Brother Ponce was exercising his role, the Founder was at the same time anxious to study for himself the situation which was developing south of the Loire, and decided to go there in person. Neither the difficulties nor the dangers of the journey would hold him back. Along roads that skirted the edges of precipices, and in mountain passes covered by thick forests, there lurked robbers and bandits of all kinds, without mention of the fanatical hatred of the Huguenots for Catholic priests.

He set out in February 1711, revisiting the communities of Moulins, Grenoble, Avignon, Alès, Mende, Marseilles. Everywhere the Brothers welcomed him with great joy; everywhere he was received by the local civil and ecclesiastical notables.

In traversing these regions, which were unknown to him, he came to realise that, given the particularities of customs and speech, the Institute could only be planted there on one incontrovertible condition: the establishment of a novitiate to provide pupils with masters of similar origin. He was turning this project over in his mind when bad news demanded his prompt return to Paris. By the end of September, he was once more settled in his community which, along with the novitiate, was installed in the rue de la Barouillère, a street which today has the honour of bearing his name.

Julien-Antoine Clement

The father of the Abbé de St Calais, Julien-Antoine Clement, was a surgeon at Court. It was he who had assisted at the lying-in of the Dauphine. He had operated on the King for a fistula. Royal gratitude was not slow in forthcoming, and in August 1711 the medical practitioner was raised to the nobility. His social advancement, following close on that of his son, gave new impetus to his ambitions. He now had a rank to maintain, to which he would devote all his energy and all his fortune. No longer was there any question of wasting money in charitable works which, no matter how deserving, would bring him no return. The first sacrifice to his vanity would be the Founder .

On 23 January 1712, he had De La Salle summoned to appear before the civil lieutenant of Le Chatelet. 'The plaintiffs' suit went as far as to accuse him of suborning a minor and extorting funds. On 17 February the Chancellery delivered to the Clements letters of rescission annulling the engagements of the Abbé, who three days later requested confirmation of these letters from Le Chatelet'.[18] Not only would he not have to make any reimbursement to the Founder, but he would, moreover, be able to claim 'restitution of the amounts which he had already drawn upon the account of the young cleric for the maintenance of the pupil-teachers.'[19] Only it was not known that, between these two events, probably on 18 February, De La Salle had left Paris and had headed south, leaving the task of coping with the likely difficulties to Brother Barthélemy, the Director of the Novitiate.

Thirty months of distancing himself

This second stay in the South, following the pattern of the launching of his previous one, was intended to complete what had until then been a simple 'making contact' as Rigault says.[20] But the developments of the Clement affair, so heavy in their consequences, were to change its whole direction to the point of making it a way of the cross.

We know the various stages which marked his journey but the absence of documentation does not permit us to determine the exact dates. Three towns were to be the scene of the most significant events

Mende

After Moulins and Avignon, he took about two months to pass through the region by Alès, Les Vans and Gravières. 'He crossed the mountains of Gevaudan at great peril and almost by miracle escaped on several occasions from losing his life. Fortunately, he finally arrived at Mende, where the Brothers had not expected him. He paid his respects to the bishop, who esteemed him highly'.[21]

It is likely that it was in this town that he received two summonses from Le Chatelet, one for the end of the month of May following on the suit of the Clements, the other for the month of June in respect of the case brought against him on 14 March by Louis Rogier, that the house at St Denis be made over to him, the purchase of which he had signed. Not knowing what decision to make, Brother Barthélemy had forwarded them to him without any comment. Was the Founder to think that the Brothers in Paris were taking the side of his enemies?

'People in this town [Mende] were so anxious to make his acquaintance … that he was obliged to conceal the moment of his departure. He set out for Marseilles, the goal of his visit to that part of France …'[22] At the end of May he was sentenced to restore to the Clements all the money they had spent on his behalf. A second judgement, on 11 June, was equally in their favour. A third, four days later, awarded Rogier the house which served as the Seminary for Country Schoolmasters. It had to be closed. John Baptist would never again find opportunity to reopen it. Only the school continued.

Marseille

He had now arrived at Marseille. 'For some time many persons in this city were hoping to see him, and several attempts had been made to have him visit. His presence was necessary to discuss the establishment of free schools where they were needed in the different parts of the city.'[23] He took the opportunity to promote his project of a novitiate 'which was received very favourably' by Mgr Henri François-Xavier de Belzunce, 'by most of the city's pastors' and by 'many pious persons',[24] so much so that, on 15 August 1712, he went on pilgrimage to Notre Dame de la Garde with his first postulants.

He devoted the month of September to retreats for the Brothers of the neighbouring communities. Later he contemplated going to join Brother Gabriel Drolin in Rome. A first attempt, some ten months earlier, had been postponed for the establishment of the novitiate as this required his presence. But the second proposal suffered the same fate, for just as he was about to embark, the Bishop asked him to remain to work on the opening of a new school. It was then at the beginning of 1713 that an open attack suddenly burst upon him.

It came from the Jansenists, for whom he had never disguised his opposition, the consequence of his loyalty to the Pope. A defamatory libel quickly spread and reached even to the remote areas where it worked its full effect. 'People believed the evil that was said of him with no other proof than that they saw it in print.'[25] The school that had been promised him was entrusted to priests. 'Even the most resolute Brothers began to waver. Some of them abandoned the Institute.'[26] There were even 'those who did not blush to tell him that 'he had come to Provence only to destroy'.[27]

He sought refuge in his usual recourse, in solitude—that is to say in God—first at Sainte Baume during Holy Week, then in the Dominican convent of St Maximin, for more than forty days. To no avail: trials caught up with him there in the person of Brother Timothée, the bearer of crushing news. The Novitiate of Marseilles, of which he had charge, had closed down with the departure of its last recruits, and Brother Ponce, the Visitor for the South, had absconded, taking with him what little there was of the community funds.

No doubt this new betrayal wounded his heart deeply, a heart which had already bled so much at the inconstancy and cowardice of followers in whom he had placed confidence and on whose loyalty he had thought he was able to rely. However, the collapse of the novitiate brought with it other serious consequences for the Institute. It was the whole plan of its being set up in the southern provinces which was now at risk, as the Founder himself explained to Brother Gabriel Drolin in July 1712: 'men of this province are needed because of the difference between the language here and that of the rest of France'.[28]

Until now, the difficulties he had encountered related only to the internal structure of his Institute: its autonomy (to preserve which he had not hesitated to leave his native city) and the principle of gratuity (the safeguarding of which, among other reasons, had led him to establish St-Yon). But now, at Marseilles, in the Midi, the south of France, it was exterior realities which challenged him. Even if the word 'inculturation' is only of recent coinage, we know that problems of this kind have faced the Church since the day of Pentecost and the Acts of the Apostles offers abundant testimony. Thus it was necessary that, in his plan to establish a new field of pastoral endeavour, John Baptist de La Salle in his turn should feel its force. It was inevitable too that he should suffer because of it.

But the trials of 1713 took on a special aspect. In the matter of the school in the Rue de Charonne, Le Chatelet, verdict of 11 July 1704 had condemned eighteen Brothers along with himself, but the verdicts of May and June 1712 and especially the campaign against him in Marseilles, were aimed solely at him. Consequently he regarded himself as the cause of the storm which was sweeping over the Institute, as the obstacle which stood in the way of its natural development. 'He began to ask himself whether his mission really was from God, and whether a work that everybody opposed was not in fact the creation of his own spirit.'[29]

This was the most subtle and at the same time the most radical temptation for a man who in his whole life had had no other desire than to accept the will of God, as he had already confessed on 28 August 1705 to his lifelong friend, the faithful Drolin:

> As for myself, I do not like to make the first move in any endeavour, and I will not do it in Rome any more than elsewhere. I leave it to Divine Providence to make the first move and I am satisfied. When it is clear that I am acting only under the direction of Providence, I have nothing to reproach myself with. When I make the first move, it is only myself who am active, so I don't expect to see much good result; neither does God usually give the action his special blessing.[30]

Did any place now remain for him among the Brothers? He thought that for the good of the Institute he should put distance between himself and his enemies. He left Marseilles for Mende and then for Grenoble.

'For you darkness itself is light …'

The haven of respite

He arrived in Grenoble at the beginning of August 1713, at the school of St Laurence, 'where he found the Brothers living in great peace, and he decided to stay with them as long as possible. He chose for himself the most secluded place in the house where he might devote himself to mental prayer. Thus he managed to live unknown and almost forgotten for the several months he was there, neither receiving nor paying calls. He did not leave his room except to attend the regular exercises at the proper times'.[31]

He continued to be concerned, however, about the situation which his absence was occasioning in Paris. At the beginning of the school year in October, he sent Brother Jacques, the Director, as his delegate while replacing him in class. When he returned in December, De La Salle learned that Brother Barthelemy, for the want of clear instructions, had not been able to prevent M. de Brou, the successor of M. Bricot as 'ecclesiastical superior', giving some reality and meaning to his title which the Brothers continued resolute in recognizing only in a purely formal sense.

Assistant priest at St-Sulpice, M. de Brou was in full accord with the views of M. de la Chétardie who wanted the schools to be under the control of the parish clergy and the Brothers who worked in them to be set up as parish associations. Other ecclesiastical superiors had already been appointed in the provinces, in particular Blain at Rouen, and there were moves afoot to insert a modification to this effect in the text of the Rule.

Strong in his resolution to keep his distance from the capital and not give it any news of himself, De La Salle, even if his role as Superior was not officially recognized by the religious authorities of Paris, continued to exercise his responsibility by forwarding obediences for vacant positions. As for deciding on his own fate, he was waiting until God would give a sign.

The Mountain of the Lord

He suffered a new bout of rheumatism in March 1714. Once again he submitted to the treatment of Dr Helvetius which exposed him on a kind of grill to the vapours of burning aromatic herbs. He came out of this treatment cured but much weakened. Jean d'Yse de Saleon, Canon of St-André of Grenoble, who had great regard for him, suggested to him that he should spend his convalescence in his house at Malesnes, at the foot of the hill of Parmenie, 'situated some four leagues from Grenoble'.[32]

On the top of the hill there was a small chapel and two groups of buildings reserved one for men and the other for women who came there for retreats. The whole place had been established in 1681 on the ruins of an old Charterhouse, by a local peasant woman who had long lived there in a kind of hermitage. She was known as Sister Louise. 'The almost continual prayer … which was her usual occupation filled her with extraordinary inspiration from heaven, and she received a particular gift for knowing the future. People came from many places to consult with her as with a prophetess and her words were regarded as oracles'.[33]

In 1714 she was 68 years old, John Baptist 63. She spoke only *patois*, he only French. But the Holy Spirit easily dispenses with language. 'De La Salle explained to her his desire to spend the rest of his life in solitude, something for which he had always felt a great attraction. The Sister replied that it was not according to God's will that he should neglect the care of his Institute. God had destined him for this work, and it was His will that he should persevere in it until the end of his days. He accepted this reply as though it were a decision rendered by God Himself.'[34]

And God confirms it

A letter arrived from Paris to confirm the word of Sister Louise. Dated 1 April (Easter Sunday 1714) it took ten days to reach him. It read:

Our very dear Father,

We, the principal Brothers of the Christian Schools, having in view the greater glory of God, the greater good of the Church and our Society , recognize that it is of the utmost importance that you should again take up the care and general government of the holy work of God, which is also yours, since it has pleased the Lord to make use of you to establish it and to direct it for such a long time. Everyone is convinced that God gave you and still gives you the graces and talents to govern properly this new Society which is so useful to the Church; and it is only just for us to acknowledge that you have always governed it with much success and edification. This is why we humbly beseech you and command you in the name of and on behalf of this Society to which you have promised obedience, to resume without delay the general government of our Society .

In testimony whereof we have signed, done at Paris, this first day of April, 1714. We are with most profound respect, our dear Father, your humble and obedient inferiors.[35]

'De La Salle was struck with astonishment on reading this letter. Various conflicting thoughts ran through his mind, leaving him undecided for a time.'[36] But recognizing the signatures, he could have no doubts.

At different times, in order to explain his thinking, to make clear his intentions, to formulate a request or to present his defence, he had addressed *Mémoires* to those concerned. More than once, too, the Brothers who kept their right to speak freely with him had had recourse to the same procedure to draw his attention to some difficult problem and to invite, even suggest, a way out.

Here it was quite different: the demand which the writers of this letter expressed did not concern a particular community but rather the whole of the Society and it was not restricted to a simple request but took the character of a duly authorized order. Clearly, something had changed in the relationships which bound the signatories to the Founder.

First of all, who were these 'principal Brothers'? The biographers do not give us their names. Maillefer simply says 'the superiors of the communities of Paris, St-Denis, and Versailles and several of the older members of the Institute',[37] that is, those who now for a long time had been members of the

Institute, companions and faithful followers of John Baptist De La Salle from the very beginning.

Next, whom did they represent? Spokesmen though they might be for their own communities, what was there to justify their belief that they were also such for all the others as their initiative might lead us to think? Nothing in their juridical position gave them any right to speak in the name of the Institute. However, they took it on themselves to do so and the terms they employed show that they were moved by a reality which went beyond themselves, an awareness of belonging to a new group which, in investing them with the same service, imposed itself upon all of them and created among them, in a very intimate fashion, a true sharing of life, thought and action. And what was this *esprit de corps* from which they drew strength and legitimacy, if not 'association'?

They were not aware of the first form association had taken in 1691, a secret close-kept by the three involved, and which would be revealed only in 1733 in the biography by Blain, five years after the return to France of Brother Gabriel Drolin, 'the last survivor'.[38] On the contrary, they attached themselves to that which defined the heart of the formula of vows by which, each year since 1694, new members committed themselves to the Institute and helped it grow.

In this supreme instance, association, which they considered to be its basis and binding cement, was found in the Body of the Institute. The authors of the letter did not claim to constitute it but they knew it existed and that that they could appeal to it. They knew that in these exceptional circumstances they should.

And since, as we have seen, the vow of obedience could be interpreted as the incarnation and one of the practical consequences of association, there was nothing surprising that they should return to it and appeal to it. Incongruous though it may seem to us, this expression 'and we order you', nailed like a flag at the top of the text, was clearly completely logical.

'Having in view the greater glory of God, the greater good of the Church and of our Society' (two different ways of saying the same thing!) John Baptist's correspondents remind him of two important facts: on the one hand, his charism of founder ('God's holy work which is also yours'; 'the Lord has made use of you to establish it and to guide it. God has given and continues to give you all the graces and talents necessary to govern this new Society'); on the other hand, his constant fidelity to this same charism ('for so long a time'; 'You have always guided it with great success and edification').

Once these two truths are brought out clearly, all that remains to be done is to return to the purpose of the letter as set out in the very beginning—'It is of the utmost importance that you resume the care and general direction ...'—and in order to end with exceptional force: 'to assume immediately the general direction of our Society.'

John Baptist de La Salle, himself also of an essentially logical mentality, for all that he was man of faith, could not fail to understand this language, a language made for him, a language modelled on his own.

Those who spoke to him of 'the holy work of God' were not aware as yet of the manuscript which, after his death, they would find among his papers, and on which he had noted a series of resolutions most likely taken, in the course of a retreat which may be dated to 1685 or 1686. There may be read this eighth article:

> I will always look upon the work of my salvation, and the foundation and government of our community, as the work of God,. hence, I will abandon the care of both to Him, acting only through his orders; and I will much consult Him upon what I have to do for the one and the other. I will often repeat the words of the prophet Habacuc: '*Domine opus tuum*' [Lord, it is thy work!].[39]

Such a correspondence of wording, as exceptional as it obvious, shows more than mere imitation, rather a hidden but real osmosis of sentiment, without which it can hardly be explained.

If, however, reading between the lines of this letter, there appears as it were in outline a new aspect of the Brothers, now more aware of themselves, more responsible, more 'grown up', there may also be discerned a more delicate portrait of the Founder seen in his double role of Father and Brother. The first—the Father—is greeted at the beginning of the letter and more solemnly still in its conclusion ('We are with the most profound respect, our dear Father, your humble and obedient inferiors'); he is also addressed thus: 'we very humbly beseech you'. But then immediately the phrase 'and we command you' looks to the second role—the Brother—who is given orders 'in the name and on behalf of this Society to which you have promised obedience'.

It is in fact on this vow of obedience that the whole unusual nature and seriousness of the situation rests. They have pronounced it, he as well as they, and from within its requirements they can in all justice address him not as equal to equal but as Brother to Brother. Already one should be able to see as it were on the horizon the outline of an intention which John Baptist had for a long time now fostered, that there be a Brother, a layman, at the head of the Brothers.

It was this constitution, typical of the Institute but as yet untried in the Church, which the members of the clergy of Paris rejected. Few though they were, they were well placed, and taking advantage of the uncertainty of Brother Barthélemy, helpless by reason of the absence of the Founder, they had succeeded in having the famous 'ecclesiastical Superiors' appointed for each community in Paris and in the provinces. The more perceptive Brothers, and especially those more under threat, saw in this the danger of fragmentation and thus of death. For the Institute to cease being what it was would be simply to cease to be at all. It was to counter this possibility that they had written.

We cannot doubt that John Baptist De La Salle was happy to see his followers take responsibility, at their own level and in their own way, for the interests of the Society, to the point of requiring him once more to take charge of them, having regard to his role in the Society .

> He was undecided as to whether he should submit to orders which came from so strange a jurisdiction. But after thinking it over he believed that he should submit without further hesitation … and that after having taught obedience for such a long time he now ought to practise it.[40]

However, it seems that the argument which influenced him most could have been the signs of esteem and attachment so warmly expressed: 'Every one is convinced'; 'It is just for us to acknowledge.' He wished to have it confirmed by all the other members of the Institute. 'Brother Barthélemy wrote to inform them of the matter and placed in his letter a copy of that of the Brothers of Paris who had recalled M. De La Salle so that all might sign it.[41] None of the original documents have come down to us.

The Third Sign

The Founder had to delay his departure some several weeks in order to attend to the case of a young man of 23 who had been recommended to him, Claude Francois du Lac de Montisambert. Born in the diocese of Orleans, in 1691 (the year of the heroic vow), his father had intended him for a military career. Having been wounded at the battle of Malplaquet in 1709, he was converted during his convalescence, left the army against his father's wishes and undertook a pilgrimage to Rome and Loreto. On the way, at Lyon and at Grenoble, he took on the care of the poor and the sick in the poor houses. He was, in fact, looking for a religious order which would accept him and he went in turn from the Capuchins in Grenoble to the monastery of the Grande Chartreuse and finally to that of the Trappists at Sept-Fons. However he could not be admitted there without the consent of his father who had mounted a search for him in France, in Switzerland and in Italy. Claude refused to ask him for anything so as not to let his whereabouts be known.

At the end of a retreat at Parmenie, 'M. de Saleon suggested him to M. De La Salle as a suitable subject for his Institute'. John Baptist put him to the test by confining him to his room for several days. He spent his time in prayer and pious reading, at the end of which time, on 6 May, he received the habit and the name of Brother Irenée.

The Founder was not to know that this new recruit would by his 'virtues shed glory on the Society and do great good there' as Director of the Novitiate and later as Assistant, before dying in a saintly manner on 3 October 1747. For the moment, he saw in him simply a proof that God was continuing to bless the Institute and wished its further development.

Return

At the beginning of June, John Baptist left Grenoble for Avignon. On the 29th of the same month occurred the death at Paris of M. de la Chétardie, the parish priest of St- Sulpice who had been so opposed to him. His itinerary took him the following month by Mende, Les Vans and Lyon to bring him by mid-July to Dijon. Finally, after a detour to Rheims, he arrived in Paris on 10 August and presented himself to the community of the Rue de la Barouillère saying, 'Here I am. What do you want of me?'[42]

A fortnight later, he learned of the death of M. Antoine Brenier, a Sulpician priest and Visitor of his Congregation, who 'was his great enemy who for ten years had been striving to take from the Servant of God the government of the Institute he had created and whose only purpose was to force him to go back to Rheims with the Brothers there so that he himself could take control of those in Paris'.[43] Quite decidedly the skies above the Institute were clearing.

Blain, whose passionate triumphalism never rejoices more than at the sight of divine justice crushing the agents of Evil, thus winds up the story of Jean-Charles Clement: 'It is not to be wondered at if this priest, who was responsible for all the disasters which we have described, came to an evil end. After the death of Philip of Orleans, the Regent, he was accused of plotting against the state and was exiled in chains far from Paris'.[44]

Lasallian texts

A clerical proposal for the Institute

The purpose was to suppress in the Institute certain customs and practices and to give it another form of government with new rules and new Superiors.

Under this proposed system

• the Brothers should have superiors from outside the Community, men capable of directing them something like the external superiors who direct nuns;

• the house in Paris should form a separate entity and should depend entirely on the ecclesiastical superior;

• the Novitiate should be suppressed as a useless burden; it cost too much to educate and feed all the novices; moreover, there was no need for so many in Paris, since the Brothers should remain fixed in the schools where they taught;

• the Brothers should stay in one place and not be changed from house to house;

• to fill the gaps made by those who died or left or who had to be dismissed for misconduct, it was proposed to have one, two or three novices, more or less, according to its revenues and its personnel needs;

• finally, a new form of government was to be set up.[45]

The Lasallian model

One faith where salvation is contemplated;
one ministry where salvation is worked out;
one community where salvation is begun.

This formula expresses the Lasallian charism as much as its spirituality:

• Charism is in the order of action, spirituality in the order of being.

• Charism envisages a manner of acting, a specific involvement, a role, with its requirements for formation, of devotion and of fidelity.

• Spirituality gives rise to a manner of being, a way of being present to others, where the deepest convictions and motivations make themselves evident.

• They are inseparable, they reciprocally correspond and interpenetrate and enliven each other, for it is the practice of the charism which develops the spirituality but at the same time it is the spirituality which makes action charismatic.

• Through faith, profession becomes ministry.

• Through ministry, the community becomes an apostolic cell.

Chapter 10

In the service of
the Church

1. The cornerstone

Return to St-Yon

On 1 September 1715, the Sun King went to bed for the last time. 'The death of King Louis XIV, which occurred in September of this same year, deprived De La Salle of the help which his friend, the Bishop of Chartres, had been able to get for him from the liberality of the King ... Now, at the end of this year, he was in such straitened circumstances that he felt obliged to leave Paris for Rouen, where he felt he could better maintain the noviti-ate.'[1]

A month later he himself came and took up residence in St-Yon. 'The task which he preferred in the house was the direction of the novices. In the past he had always made that his best loved occupation and his principal duty ... What he was after was holiness, not numbers.'[2]

Two benefactors from Calais and Boulogne came one day to visit him there. In the course of the meal, they expressed astonishment that he should have undertaken a work so useful to the Church but at the same time bris-tling with so many difficulties. He replied in a confidential manner, 'If God had told me what sufferings and crosses were to accompany the establishing of this Institute, at the same time as he was showing me the good it would do, my courage would have failed me. I would not have dared to touch it with the tip of my fingers.'[3]

He had, however, to put the finishing touches to this task. 'He saw himself advanced in years, and he feared that after his death the Brothers would find it very difficult to elect one of their own for Superior General. He knew from experience the trouble he had to preserve the Institute from being governed by strangers who several times had been forced upon the Brothers. He foresaw that if he could not prevent this from happening in the future, he would have to anticipate relaxation creeping in, and as a necessary consequence, the loss of all the fruit he had hoped for from his Society'.[4]

In November 1716, he managed to convince the Brothers in St-Yon and Rouen. They accepted his plan for a general Assembly which would relieve him of the Superiorship and thus would bring to its completion the organisation of the Institute. They also decided that, to enable the Communities to understand the situation clearly, the best means would be to send them one of their own number who would set out all the facts in detail and who would be able, for greater clarity, to answer their questions. They chose Brother Barthélemy. Leaving in early December, he returned from his journey across France only in March 1717, bearing the agreement of everybody.

The second general Chapter

The second General Chapter opened on 16 May, Pentecost Sunday. Sixteen capitulants represented the hundred or so Brothers who then made up the Society. John Baptist de La Salle pointed out the great importance of the action on which they were embarking. Then, after refusing the presidency of the Assembly, he withdrew to his room so as not to have any influence on the openness of the discussions.

On 18 May, they proceeded to the election of the Superior. The choice fell on Brother Barthélemy and when the news was announced to the Founder, he replied without surprise, 'he has been acting as such for a long time'.[5]

An essential stage had just been completed by the Institute. Existing only through the free association of its members, it derived its legitimacy only from itself. It was also from within itself that it was to draw its own government, whence the responsibility for wanting at its head only one of its own subjects

This election brought the final touch to its internal structure. It assured its autonomy, in jeopardy for so long, and which ran the greatest risk under ecclesiastical supervision. Above all it established in an unquestionable way its identity, the characteristic features it was acquiring and the distinctive place it aspired to in the Church. It would remain for the Church only to confirm these, eight years later, by means of its official approbation, thus dispelling in a definitive manner all the ambiguities which had vitiated its existence in the parishes and dioceses, as well as its relationships with parish priests and bishops. It would be for the Institute an authentic guarantee of permanence.

It would also be for the Church itself the emergence of a new manner of being and of thinking about itself. In the Institute, indeed, it already existed as the 'People of God', defined and recognised first and foremost in a mission in which the promotion of justice pursued as an intrinsic element of evangelisation; as the 'Body of Christ', in which the inexhaustible divine richness is manifest through the many charisms which bring up to date the ministries traditional in the work for salvation; and as 'one Flock' in which the laity finds its full place, in which the hierarchy substitutes for consciousness of status the sense of service, in which the magisterium takes on, more than anything, the role of authenticating the Spirit in its many manifestations, guaranteeing their originality. This was a Church, in short, nearer to Vatican II than to the Council of Trent. A Church in which, on principle, dominating behaviour would no longer become possible such as the effort at control exercised for many years contrary to the interests of the Society.

At the express request of the newly elected Superior, the Chapter again designated Brothers John and Joseph, directors of the houses in Paris and Rheims, 'who would be named Assistants of the Brother Superior ... and who would help him with their advice' (Acts of the Chapter). From that time on, custom gave Brother Barthélemy first place on the list of the Superior Generals, reserving to John Baptist de La Salle the title 'Founder'. In this way the totally lay character of the Institute was insisted on.

The Assembly continued to fulfil its mandate by revising the text of the *Rules* and the *Conduct of Schools*. It finished on 23 May, the feast of the Holy Trinity, with the ceremony of vows.

2. What did this mean for De La Salle?

The status of inferior

Relieved of business matters, De La Salle kept to his humble and docile position as expressed in two letters he subsequently addressed to Brother Barthélemy: 'You know that I am always ready to obey you in everything since I am subject to your authority, and I did not vow obedience to do what I like'.[6] 'If I am to be considered a member of the Brothers of the Christian Schools, it seems to me that my present position ought to be one of simple submission and that I should make no move in what concerns them except through obedience'.[7]

The work

Eager 'to spend the rest of his life in solitude, something for which he had always felt a great attraction', as he had confided to Sister Louise, he looked upon her response 'as though it were a decision rendered from God Himself', namely that God 'had destined him for this work, and it was His will that he should persevere in it until the end of his days'.[8] As a consequence, he applied himself to two writings which were to crown his work as founder and which would be published with others after his death.

In the first, *Explanation of the Method of Interior Prayer*, he synthesises the teachings he gave to the novices on the subject of mental prayer. Although he sought to generalise them for all the Brothers, the book bears the marks of the condition of those for whom it was first destined, whose interior life, Blain tells us, he was especially careful to perfect, 'convinced that the holiness of his Institute depended on the fervour of the novices'.[9]

Likewise there is no doubt that in it he poured out, under the veil of a very assured knowledge of the ways of the spiritual life, the secrets of his own union with God. Whence the quasi-mystical aspect of these lines that could seem to have been written for contemplatives. They are offered in such a way that they bear witness to the constant preoccupation of John Baptist to inspire his Brothers with a sincere and profound desire for intimacy with God in order to ensure the greatest possible fruit in their apostolate for souls.

Let us not forget, on the other hand, that the texts of the Founder make up an inseparable whole whose multiple facets reflect, the richness of the Lasallian vocation. It would be a grave mistake to read them in isolation one from another, to take any single one of them as the integral expression of his thinking, to consider, for example, that the whole of his spirituality is found enclosed in the *Collection*. Let us be on our guard lest we take one flower for the whole bouquet.

The second text to which the Founder gave the final touches in the same period comes just at the right moment to corroborate this remark. While he integrates in the spiritual life of the Brothers their professional and apostolic activity, in contrast he separates from it the community dimension.

Its title, *Meditations for the Time of Retreat*, is completed by the following information: 'For the use of all persons engaged in the education of youth and, particularly for the retreat which the Brothers of the Christian Schools make during vacation'.

This book, then, is written for the Brothers, but not for them alone. It is meant also for all the other Gospel workers who, whether men or women, priests or lay persons, share in the same school apostolate but do not live in community, and this explains the lack of reference to this domain. Among them, John Baptist includes, certainly, his former 'teachers for country schools' for whom he kept all his affection. And, if it would be too much to pretend that he may have foreseen the present situation in which so many of the Brothers' helpers, Lasallians in mind and heart, share their mission, what an updating, nevertheless, of his thought!

In this text, the word 'education' is not qualified by 'Christian', contrary to the most frequent usage of the author. There can be no doubt, however, that, in his mind, the adjective goes without saying, as he showed by numerous examples throughout all his written works and as he witnessed wholeheartedly throughout his whole life and action.

He has left texts of various kinds: spiritual, catechetical or pedagogical, each bringing it own illumination. It can be said without exaggeration that the *Meditations for the Time of Retreat* provide the key to them: not only do they give evidence of their essential cohesion, but, in addition, they complete their impact by opening them up to the Institute's lay partners.

In these meditations John Baptist de La Salle offers a synthesis of his thought, his experience and his life. It is a solidly built synthesis and develops by rigorous steps. Unfortunately their form makes access arduous for contemporary readers, stemming mainly from their grammatical structure. Their long, complex sentences linked together and stuffed with incidentals with multiple logical implications are disconcerting to modern intellectual habits and our use of a language which, since then, has evolved so much.[10]

Three themes, among others, are going to receive our attention

— the unity of Lasallian life;

— the building up of the Church;

— the inspiration and power of the Spirit.

'State' and 'employment'

'The obligations of community life and their school duties demand their entire time and energy.'[11] Such is the first formulation that John Baptist de La Salle gives of the unity of life of his disciples in the *Memoir on the Habit*. To express the same idea, he also makes use of two terms which, linked together or not, recur very commonly from his pen.

The first, 'state', refers to the particular situation of the Brother in the Church: that of an unmarried man, a layman, associated by vow with other Brothers to live in community with them and to keep, always with them, Christian schools in view of allowing the young, especially the poor, to have access to the Good News and, through that, to salvation. That notion is enriched today with the religious character which it did not possess at the start but which in the recent past the Church recognises as the Institute's.

In the second, 'employment', he indicates the specific activity of the Brother, a profession raised to the rank of a ministry (note that the two words share the same Latin etymology), that is, extending the strictly professional functions (lessons, corrections, supervision, personal and social formation) by means of preoccupations of the pastoral order (catechism, Christian initiation, the practice of prayer and the sacraments). It is important to keep in mind the fact that these two fields of action, far from existing in separate areas, blend into a single commitment, since it is from the very heart of the first that the second is exercised and flourishes.

But just as the Founder's synthetic mind had inseparably tied together human and Christian education (one could also say 'culture and faith' or 'development and evangelisation'), likewise has he established an essential connection between *state* and *employment*. The apostolic ministry of the Brother is the necessary extension of his religious life, which finds in it its reason and its opportunity. It inspires it as it embodies it. It expresses it as it requires it.

In the thought of the Founder, the close joining together of state and employment, highlights in each of them two major elements of Lasallian life: zeal and prayer. That prayer is part of the religious life of the Brother does not have to be proved. And to prove that it applies also to the work, it is sufficient to go back to the fourth and eighth *Meditations for the Time of Retreat*:

> You must, then, devote yourself very much to prayer in order to succeed in

your ministry. You must constantly represent the needs of your disciples to Jesus Christ, explaining to him the difficulties you have experienced in guiding them. Jesus Christ, seeing that you regard him as the one who can do everything in your work and yourself as an instrument that ought to be moved only by him, will not fail to grant you what you ask of him.[12]

You, then, who have succeeded the apostles in their work of catechising and instructing the poor, if you want to make your ministry as useful to the Church as it can be, you must, every day, teach them catechism, helping them to learn the basic truths of our religion, following the example of the apostles, which is that of Jesus Christ himself, who devoted himself every day to this task.

Like them, also, you must afterwards withdraw in order to devote yourselves to reading and prayer, to instruct yourselves thoroughly in the truths and the holy maxims which you wish to teach, and to draw upon yourselves by prayer the grace of God that you need to do this work according to the Spirit and the intentions of the Church, which entrusts it to you.[13]

Zeal, an essential factor in the work, we find linked with state in the two following extracts:

What ought to engage you further to have great zeal in your state is the fact that you are not only the ministers of God, but also of Jesus Christ and of the Church.[14]

You can expect yet another reward which God will give you in advance in this life if you devote yourselves generously to your duty and, if through zeal and the grace of your state, you have known well how to give your disciples a foundation in the Christian spirit.[15]

Certainly, the idea expressed here takes on a peculiar force from the insertion into the sentence of the word 'state'. But would the meaning be very different if the word 'employment' replaced it?

As we have seen, concern for a serious and sustained Christian way of living is indispensable for the Lasallian teacher for his labours to bear fruit. And by a kind of boomerang effect, the very concern he has for the salvation of his disciples increases grace in him and causes him to make progress in sanctity. This is the theme of the thirteenth *Meditation for the Time of Retreat*:

Consider that the account you will have to give to God will not be inconsequential, because it concerns the salvation of the souls of children whom

God has entrusted to your care, for on the day of judgement you will answer for them as much as for yourself.

You must be convinced of this, that God will begin by making you give an account of their souls before making you give an account of your own ...

This is what Saint Paul brings to your attention, when he says that those who have been put in charge of others must render an account of them to God (Hebrews 13:17).

The basic reason for this is, that when they carry out well the service of guides and leaders of the souls entrusted to them, they fulfil at the same time their own duties towards God. God will fill them with so much grace that they themselves will be made holy while they are contributing as far as they are able to the salvation of others.

You have exercises which are arranged for your own sanctification, but if you have an ardent zeal for the salvation of those you are called to instruct, you will not fail to perform them and to relate them to this intention. In doing this you will draw on your students the graces needed to contribute to their salvation, and you can be assured that if you act in this way for their salvation, God himself will take responsibility for yours.[16]

'The Church of Rome'

His unswerving attachment

What focused the attention of John Baptist de La Salle, right from his earliest years, was the Church. The force that drove him throughout his life, that gave direction to his choices and drove him to the most heroic resolutions was his love for the Church and his resolve to serve it better and better. Nothing that he undertook to defend it seemed to him beyond his strength so great was the primary concern of his heart to remain always faithful to it. In this instance, his biographers show themselves to be precious and irrefutable witnesses.

When his parents approved his priestly vocation, 'What joy filled John Baptist's heart when he saw himself free to follow his desires, which, ever since he could remember, had urged him to devote himself to the service of God! What happiness was his when he realised he could enter a state which would enrol him officially in the service of the Church!'[17] He then received the tonsure: 'this appeared to him as a worthy motive for loving the Church'.[18]

After his ordination, 'Roland ... told him that in the service of the Church he should not seek a sinecure but should be willing to seek out a more difficult assignment … He felt that he had found the opportunity, by giving his canonry to the pastor of St Peter's in Rheims'.[19] From that time, he 'thought that a parish would be a more appropriate position for him than a Canon's stall, and that as parish priest he would be more useful to the Church'.[20]

He felt subsequently that his duties as a canon did not allow him to devote himself as much as he desired to looking after the schools and the teachers. 'De La Salle's zeal felt too hemmed in by the exigencies of the canonical state. The sacred desire he experienced to serve the Church felt itself too constrained'.[21] Thus we can understand the *Te Deum* he caused to be sung once he was relieved of it, 'seeing himself freed from duties in which he looked upon himself as of little use to the Church'.[22]

The mission of salvation in the Church

The Church, as it is set before us in the *Meditations for the Time of Retreat*, is the product of the divine plan of the Covenant which embraces the whole of humanity: 'God is so good that, having created us, he wills that all of us come to the knowledge of the truth … That is why God wills all people to be instructed'.[23] 'God wills not only that all come to knowledge of truth, but also that all be saved'.[24] The Word does not justify his incarnation in any other way: 'he came on earth, as he himself said, only that people might have life and have it to the full'.[25]

He passes on this mission, which consists in announcing salvation and bringing it about, through the intermediary of the Apostles, to the Church: 'This truth is God himself and what he has desired to reveal to us through Jesus Christ, through the holy Apostles, and through his Church' (*MTR*, 193,1). The Church carries this out through its members whom God has set aside for himself for this purpose, 'this is what God does by diffusing the fragrance of his teaching throughout the whole world by human ministers'.[26] 'God who has established in the Church apostles, prophets and teachers.'[27]

By means of the Christian school

This introduction includes nothing that is not traditional. What is least traditional is the quiet boldness and the strength of the language with which John Baptist de La Salle considers the Brothers equivalent to the Church's ministers. To express the apostolic activity of his disciples, he in fact uses the word 'ministry' nineteen times and he has already used it thirty-four times, for the same purpose, in the *Meditations for Sundays and Feasts*.

The texts here are conclusive. For example:

> Reflect on what Saint Paul says that it is God who has established in the Church apostles, prophets and teachers, and you will be convinced that he has also established you in your work.[28]

> You are not only ministers of God but also of Jesus Christ and of the Church. This is what Saint Paul says when he expresses the wish that everyone should regard those who announce the Gospel as ministers of Jesus Christ, who write the letter which he has dictated not with ink but with the Spirit of the living God, not on tablets of stone but on tablets of flesh which are the hearts of children.[29]

To avoid multiplying quotations, let us limit ourselves to Meditation 193, suggested for the morning of the first day of retreat. It bears the title 'That God in his Providence has established the Christian Schools'. It could be sub-titled 'The place of the Christian school in the pastoral activity of the Church'.

It presents the proclamation of salvation, firstly in the framework of the parish (1st point) then in the more particular one of the family (2nd point) keeping for the 3rd the question of its fulfilment. But what seems to us most characteristic (and most enlightening about the intentions of the author), is the fact that the three points are built up on the same framework

1. John Baptist begins by demonstrating the obligation for the Church to carry the message, 'We cannot be instructed in the mysteries of our holy religion unless *we have the good fortune to hear about them,* and we cannot have this advantage unless someone preaches the word of God.'

Equivalently, it is to be deplored that 'fathers and mothers' far from 'bringing up their children in a Christian manner', 'cannot take the time to teach their children their duties as Christians' (the situation will be treated in detail in the following meditation, for the afternoon of the same day).

At the same time he puts forward the argument that God 'wills that all be saved. He cannot truly desire this without providing the means for it'.

2. With this background pertaining to the Church, the parents and God, he then introduces the Lasallian vocation:

> This is what God does by diffusing the fragrance of his teaching throughout the whole world by human ministers. Just as he commanded light to shine out of darkness, so he himself kindles a light in the hearts of those destined to announce his word to children, so that they may be able to enlighten

those children by unveiling for them the glory of God.

It is characteristic of the providence of God and of his vigilance over human conduct to substitute for fathers and mothers persons who have enough knowledge and zeal to bring children to the knowledge of God and of his mysteries. According to the grace of Jesus Christ, that God has given to them, they are like good architects who give all possible care and attention to lay the foundation of religion and Christian piety in the hearts of these children, a great number of whom would otherwise be abandoned.

… and, without giving children the teachers who will assist them in the fulfilment of his plan. This, says Saint Paul, is the field that God cultivates, the building that he is raising, and you are the ones whom he has chosen to help in this work by announcing to these children the Gospel of his Son and the truths that are contained in it.

3. In a few very compressed words, he declares three times that this vocation constitutes a ministry in the Church:

Since, then, God in his mercy has given you such a ministry …

You, then, whom God has called to this ministry …

This is why you must honour your ministry.

4. He states that this ministry displays the specific characteristic of fitting into the context of a profession and including therein a triple duty:

— to transmit the Word to children: '
do not falsify his word but gain glory before him by unveiling his truth to those whom you are charged to instruct. Let this be your whole effort in the instructions you give them.

— to form them to the Christian life:
work according to the grace that has been given to you to instruct by teaching and to exhort by encouraging those who are entrusted to your care, guiding them with attention and vigilance.

— to lead them in the ways of salvation:
keep trying to save some of these children. Since God, according to the expression of the same Apostle, has made you his ministers in order to reconcile them to him and he has entrusted to you for this purpose the word of reconciliation for them, exhort them, then, as if God were exhorting them through you, for you have been destined to cultivate these young plants by announcing to them the truths of the Gospel, and to procure for them the means of salvation appropriate to their development.

Teach them these truths, not with learned words, lest the cross of Christ, source of our salvation, become void of meaning and all you say to them would produce no fruit in their minds or hearts.'

5. Finally he gives titles under whose banner the Lasallian teacher acts:
— Ministers of God and Dispensers of his Mysteries
— Substitutes for Fathers and Mothers
— Instruments of salvation.

It was an idea dear to John Baptist de La Salle that vocation confers on those who are called certain titles (usually spelt with a capital), but it is dependent on those people to conform their life, their sentiments and their course of action to these titles.

Within humanity to be saved, within the Church, he singles out children to whom alone he becomes attached and to whose service he assigns apostles specially trained for them. He stresses in turn their being chosen by God as 'those destined to announce his word' (1st point), their quality of 'persons who have enough knowledge and zeal' (2nd point), and finally their professional name 'teachers' (3rd point). Likewise as he went along he specified their competencies: 'to announce his word to children' (1st point), 'to bring children to the knowledge of God and of his mysteries' (2nd point), to 'assist them in the fulfilment of his plan [that all may be saved]'(3rd point).

As for the ministry, it is developed by way of a constant exchange, of constant transition. God showers his gifts on the teacher so that he may transmit them to his disciples with a reflex action back to the teacher, in view of his personal sanctification:

— destined to announce his word to children ... he has entrusted to you for this purpose the word of reconciliation for them ... do not falsify his word.

— he himself kindles a light in the hearts of those destined to announce his word to children, so that they may be able to enlighten those children.

— by unveiling for them the glory of God ... gain glory before him by unveiling his truth to those whom you are charged to instruct.

This glory provided his last word in the book, since it concludes Meditation 208, foreseen for the afternoon of the eighth and last day of the retreat.

The Body and the Sanctuary

In order to initiate the first Christians into the mystery of the Church, St Paul often had recourse to two images, those of the body and the building.

This latter will become moreover so significant that the word meaning the assembly of the faithful will very soon be applied to the place of the worship which united them.

John Baptist makes use of these images even from the first Meditation in which he introduces Lasallian teachers who, 'according to the grace of Jesus Christ, that God has given to them, are like good architects who give all possible care and attention to lay the foundation of religion and Christian piety in the hearts of these children, a great number of whom would otherwise be abandoned'.[30]

He develops his thought and states with the greatest clarity:

> You should be working in your ministry for the building of the Church on the foundation which has been laid by the holy apostles by the instruction you are giving to the children whom God has entrusted to your care and who are entering into the construction of this building (*MTR*, 200, 1).

> This means that you are called to lay the foundation for the building of the Church when you instruct children in the mystery of the most Holy Trinity and the mysteries accomplished by Jesus Christ (*MTR*, 199, 1).

> In making you responsible for the instruction of children and their formation in piety, Jesus Christ entrusted to you the task of building up his body which is the Church. You are likewise responsible, as far as you are able, to make her holy, and to purify her by the word of life, so that she may be able to appear before him full of glory without stain, without wrinkle, and without any defect, but completely pure and completely beautiful (*MTR*, 205, 3).

The love of the Lasallian teacher for the Church is manifest in the zeal he displays in its service:

> You must also show the Church what love you have for her and give her proof of your zeal, since it is for the Church (which is the body of Jesus Christ) that you work. You have become her ministers according to the order God has given you to dispense his word ... so that you can say to God as the holy King David, the zeal of your house has consumed me. For this house is none other than the Church, since the faithful form this building which has been built on the foundation of the apostles, and raised up by Jesus Christ who is the main cornerstone (*MTR*, 201, 2).

These same words, this same quotation from the Epistle of St Paul to the Ephesians (5:25-27), are applied with as much assurance for the benefit of the children:

Act in such a way through your zeal that you give tangible proof that you love those whom God has entrusted to you, just as Jesus Christ has loved his Church. Help them enter truly into the structure of this building, and be in a position to appear one day before Jesus Christ full of glory, without stain, without wrinkle, without blemish (*MTR*, 201, 2).

It is not unintentionally that he emphasises his idea by using the adverb 'truly' in the extent to which he requires Lasallian teachers 'to have an altogether special esteem for the Christian instruction and education of children, since it is a means of helping them become true children of God and citizens of heaven. This is the very foundation and support of their piety and of all the other good that takes place in the Church' (*MTR*, 199, 3).

Finally, when he envisages the account the Lasallian teacher will have to render to God when he appears before him, he concludes:

The best way to be pleasing to Jesus Christ, when he judges you, will be to present to him all those children you have instructed as part of the building of the Church and have brought by your care into its structure to become the sanctuary where God dwells by the Holy Spirit (*MTR*, 205, 3).

The Field and the Vine

Speaking about himself and Apollo, St Paul writes to the Christians of Corinth: 'We are God's servants. working together; you are God's field, God's building' (1 Corinthians 3:9).

John Baptist de La Salle takes up this passage and applies it to the teachers in his schools. 'This, says Saint Paul, is the field that God cultivates, the building that he is raising, and you are the ones he has chosen to help in this work … you have been destined to cultivate these young plants by announcing to them the truths of the Gospel, and to procure for them the means of salvation appropriate to their development' (*MTR*, 193, 3). He comes back to it in the thirteenth meditation: 'You cooperate with God in his work, says Saint Paul, and the souls of the children whom you teach are the field that he cultivates through you' (*MTR*, 205, 1). Similarly, he writes in the ninth: 'It is God who has called you, who has destined you for this work, and who has sent you to work in his vineyard. Do this then, with all the affection of your heart, working entirely for him' (*MTR*, 201, 1).

'Be convinced of what Saint Paul says, that you plant and water the seed, but it is God through Jesus Christ who makes it grow, and brings your work to fulfilment' (*MTR*, 196, 1). Thus the principle of the pastoral fruitfulness of the teachers is set out, that is, in the terminology of John Baptist de La Salle, their 'fruit'. Now, as a work of grace, the apostolate produces its effect only through a selective intervention of God who, according to the expression of the Founder, 'gives it his blessing':

> All your care for the children entrusted to you would be useless if Jesus Christ himself did not give the quality, the power, and the efficacy that is needed to make your care useful. As the branch of the vine cannot bear fruit (our Lord says) unless it remains attached to the stem, so neither can you bear fruit, if you do not remain in me. All the good you are able to do in your work for those entrusted to you will be true and effective only insofar as Jesus Christ gives it his blessing and as you remain united with him. Jesus Christ wants you to understand from this comparison that the more the work for the good of your disciples is given life by him and draws its power from him, the more it will produce good in them. That is why you must ask him earnestly that all your instructions be given life by his Spirit and draw all their power from him. Just as he is the one who enlightens everyone coming into the world, he also is the one who enlightens the minds of your students and leads them to love and practise the good that you teach them (*MTR*, 195, 3).

To this first application that John Baptist singles out, in the morning of the second day of the Retreat, he adds a second in the afternoon: '

> Keep, then, the goals of your work as completely pure as those of Jesus Christ himself; by this means you will draw upon yourselves and all your labours his blessing and grace (*MTR*, 196, 3).

Undoubtedly, this would be the best means for obtaining, in eternity, the reward reserved for good servants as John Baptist recalls in the two meditations for the last day: 'Oh, how fortunate you ought to consider yourselves, to be working in the field of the Lord, since our Lord says that the reaper will infallibly receive his reward' (*MTR*, 207, 1). 'Consider, then, that your reward in heaven will be all the greater as you will have accomplished more good in the souls of the children who are entrusted to your care' (*MTR*, 208, 1).

That, for sure, is something to encourage us.

The Flock

Presenting the Church under the image of the flock is so traditional that the 'pastoral' concept is drawn from it. Nevertheless John Baptist de La Salle made little use of it in the *Meditations for the Time of Retreat*.

Once more he refers to St Paul who 'wrote to the Corinthians ... It is only in Jesus Christ that I lay hold to some glory for what I have done for God.' Then he comments,

> It was, then, the spread of God's glory by the preaching of the Gospel that made up all the consolation of this great apostle, and this must be yours as well, to make God and his Son Jesus Christ known to the flock confided to you (*MTR*, 207, 2).

He then proposes Jesus Christ as the perfect model for the Lasallian teacher:

> Consider Jesus Christ as the Good Shepherd of the Gospel who seeks the lost sheep, places it upon his shoulders, and carries it back to restore it to the fold. Since you are taking his place, look upon yourself as obliged to do the same thing. Ask him for the grace needed to procure the conversion of their hearts (*MTR*, 196, 1).

It is interesting to compare this text with Meditation 33 in which the Founder draws from the same scripture passage (John 10:11-16) considerations of a pedagogical nature: '

> In today's Gospel Jesus Christ compares those who have charge of souls to a good shepherd who has great care for the sheep. One quality he must possess, according to our Saviour, is to know each one of them individually [1st point]. It is also necessary, says Jesus Christ, that the sheep know their shepherd in order to be able to follow him [2nd point]. The members of the flock of Jesus Christ are also obliged to hear their shepherd's voice. It is, then, your duty to teach the children entrusted to you; this is your duty every day [3rd point].

For John Baptist de La Salle, this advice is so much more precious because it is addressed not to simple teachers, but to catechists, to apostles. Though he renewed, with a flair of genius, the art of teaching, it was not in the manner of a pedagogue concerned to make the school institution more suitable to fulfil its role: it was as a pastor who has adopted the goal of transforming the school into a milieu in which the Gospel, proclaimed, will be adopted because it is already the way of life.

Thus, there is no incompatibility between these two meditations: No. 196 simply gives No. 33 its specific meaning.

'The Spirit of God'

We have already come across this theme in the citations relating to the Church.

Indeed, how does one speak of the Church without coming, sooner or later, to the Holy Spirit? The Church is the Spouse of Christ whose Body it is, born on the cross of the blood and water which flowed from his pierced heart. After the Last Supper he had said to his Apostles, 'It is to your advantage that I go away, for if I do not go away the Advocate will not come to you; but if I go I will send him to you ... When the Spirit of truth comes, he will guide you into all the truth; for he will not speak on his own, but he will speak whatever he hear' (John 16:7-13).

Source of divine life

John Baptist de La Salle starts from the Pauline principle according to which the source of charisms and ministries in the Church is none other than the Holy Spirit:

> Reflect on what saint Paul says, that it is God who has established in the Church apostles, prophets, and teachers, and you will be convinced that he has also established you in your work. The same saint gives us another expression of this when he says that there are diverse ministries but there are different operations, and the Holy Spirit manifests himself in each of these gifts for the common good, that is to say, for the good of the Church. One receives by the Spirit the gift to speak with wisdom, another the gift of faith by the same Spirit.
>
> You must not doubt that it is a great gift of God, this grace he has given you to be entrusted with the instruction of children, to announce the Gospel to them and to bring them up in the spirit of religion (*MTR*, 201, 1).

That is what happens because it is the Spirit who, in the soul of each of the faithful, brings about conversion and sanctification. Through natural opportunities and of human instruments, the Spirit 'touches hearts', that is, makes his way into them and fills them with light and strength, in order, eventually, to transform them by establishing himself in them with the other two Persons of the Blessed Trinity.

The Founder has already informed us in his meditation for Pentecost Sunday: 'You carry out a work that requires you to touch hearts, but this you cannot do except by the Spirit of God'.[31] He returns to the point five times in the *Meditations for the Time of Retreat*, starting with the third:

> Since you are the ambassadors and ministers of Jesus Christ in the work that you do, you must act as representing Jesus Christ himself. He wants your disciples to see him in you and receive your instructions as if he were giving

them to them. They must be convinced your instructions are the truth of Jesus Christ who speaks with your mouth, that it is only in his name that you teach, and that it is he who has given you authority over them.

They must also be convinced that they themselves are a letter which Jesus Christ dictates to you, which you write each day in their hearts, not with ink, but by the Spirit of the living God, who acts in you and by you.[32]

He takes up the same citation from 2 Corinthians 3:3, with a parallel commentary in *MTR*, 201, 2.

Let us quote again:

'God has called you to your ministry in order to procure his glory and to give children the spirit of wisdom, the insight to know him, and to enlighten the eyes of their hearts ... (Ephesians 1:17-18).[33]

That is why you must ask him earnestly that all your instructions be given life by his Spirit and draw all their power from him. Just as he is the one who enlightens everyone coming into the world, he is also the one who enlightens the minds of your students and leads them to love and to practise the good that you teach them.[34]

From the pen of John Baptist de La Salle is found an expression very close to *touching hearts*, and that is *winning hearts*. *Touching hearts* conjures up the ultimate effort of God to convert a soul; *winning hearts* means simply 'to gain the confidence or even the affection of someone', in this case that of the students. If the Lasallian teacher is to try hard to do so, it is certainly not for himself but only for God:

You must consider the obligation you have to win their hearts as one of the principal means to lead them to live in a Christian manner.[35]

Again:

The gift of tongues is the ability to speak in order to attract souls to God, to procure conversion, and to tell each one what he needs to hear. For God does not win over all souls to himself by the same means; we need to know how to speak in the right way to each one of them, in order to engage them to give themselves entirely to God.[36]

These last two passages are markers in the Founder's thought on this subject. They denote the change between the 'heart' which remains in the natural domain and the 'soul' which comes under grace alone. Thus, once the behaviour of the teacher, his way of being present, his attention, his devotedness, the many signs of his love, in a word, all that the Founder calls his 'care', have 'touched the heart' of the student, the Spirit, in his turn, can 'touch' his heart and, at the same time, 'the soul is won for God'. Then, and only then, has the Christian school fulfilled its role and attained its end.

Then, and only then, can John Baptist de La Salle write in his last Meditation for the Time of Retreat, for the benefit of 'all persons engaged in the education of youth':

> Your happiness in heaven will be greater than what will be enjoyed by those who have worked only for their own salvation, and it will be much greater in proportion to the number of children you have instructed and won over to God.[37]

Condition for apostolic fruit

Since it is the Holy Spirit who brings about in each person the work of salvation, the first obligation of the Lasallian teacher is, obviously, to look upon himself and to act only as the Spirit's humble fellow worker. That in no way dispenses him from his own personal contribution by means of deepening his own Christian life and by the intensity of his pastoral commitment:

> If you want the instructions you give those whom you have to instruct to be effective in drawing them to the practice of good, you must practise these truths yourselves, and you must be full of zeal, so that your students may be able to receive a share of the grace which is in you for doing good, and that your zeal draw upon you the Spirit of God to animate your students in the same way.[38]

The teacher, who knows that he is not working for himself, must above all renounce 'his own spirit'. This is one of the effects of the spirit of faith which leads 'to doing nothing but in view of God', what is also sometimes called purity of intention:

> In order for you to fulfil this duty with as much perfection and exactness as God requires of you, frequently give yourself to the Spirit of our Lord to act in your work only under his influence, so that your own spirit may have no part in it. This Holy Spirit, then, will come upon them generously, so that they will be able to possess fully the Christian spirit.[39]

Becoming empty of self like this makes no sense unless it is to yield to God all the space, all the initiative. This real substitution of the agent is called for especially under two particular circumstances:

1. In the difficulties or obstacles met in the apostolate:

> When it happens that you encounter some difficulty in the guidance of your disciples, when there are some who do not profit from your instructions and

you observe a certain spirit of immorality in them, turn to God with confidence. Very insistently ask Jesus Christ to make his Spirit come alive in you, since he has chosen you to do his work.[40]

2. In 'corrections', which require really sure discernment more than tact. Here there is not question of evaluating a student's task, which is the meaning the word has taken on in today's language. It is, rather, the case of disciplining every violation occurring in school. For John Baptist de La Salle there is always some sinfulness at the base of these disorders (laziness, disobedience, anger, pride …) and the educational action of the teacher consists less in punishing an infringement of school regulations than of making students aware of the evil within them to bring them to correct themselves and to put them back on the right path:

> It would be of little value to make reproofs and corrections, if those who make them do not take the right steps to make them well. The first thing to which we must pay attention is not to undertake reproofs and corrections except under the guidance of the Spirit of God. That is why, before undertaking them, it is proper to become interiorly recollected, to give ourselves up to God's Spirit, and to be disposed to make the reproof or undertake the correction with the greatest possible wisdom and in a manner best suited to make them useful to the one to whom we intend to make it.
>
> For people, and even children, are endowed with reason and must not be corrected like animals, but like reasonable persons.
>
> We must reprove and correct with justice, by helping the children to recognise the wrong they have done, and what correction the wrong they have committed deserves and we must try to have them accept it.[41]

If it happens that you have been aroused by some passion, avoid making any correction while you experience this emotion, because then the correction would be very harmful to your disciples as well as to yourself. In those situations enter into yourself and allow the time of anger to pass without showing it exteriorly. Then, when you are completely free of passion, you will be able to abandon yourself to God's Spirit and make the correction you planned with all the moderation of which you are capable.[42]

However, the privileged spot, where the Spirit is active, is still that of 'instruction' or the catechism lesson:

> This must be your goal when you instruct your disciples, that they live a Christian life and that your words become spirit and life for them. Your words will accomplish this because they will be produced by the Spirit of God living in you.[43]

Life in the Spirit

It is not enough for John Baptist de La Salle that the teacher be filled with and animated by the third divine Person to the extent of becoming his 'instrument' (*MTR*, 196,1), it is also needful that his students become receptive to the reality of the Spirit. For this purpose, the Church makes use of the holy anointing which perfects baptism. The prescriptions of the Founder in this area leave no place for ambiguity:

> In imitation of the apostles you must give an altogether special care that those whom you instruct receive the sacraments, in particular that they are made ready to receive Confirmation with the proper dispositions in order to be filled with the Holy Spirit and the graces which this sacrament produces.[44]

In order that, afterwards, they live fully by it, he adds:

> You must work to inspire them with the same sentiments and to put them in the same dispositions in which Saint Paul tried to place the Ephesians through the letter he wrote to them, that they not sadden the Holy Spirit of God, with whom they have been marked in baptism and in confirmation as by a seal for the day of redemption'[45]

On that day, the teachers will be able to present them at last to Jesus Christ

> as part of the building of the Church and brought by your care into its structure to become the sanctuary where God dwells by the Holy Spirit.[46]

'God is so good'

These words which begin Meditation 193 (the first meditation of the first day of the Retreat) are recalled again at the beginning of Meditation 207 (the first of the last day). So, they open and close the Retreat. They surround it as it unfolds. They weave its background, fix its basis securely and impregnate its tone. Of the plans of God which they show, one applies to 'all men' (*MTR*, 193, 1), the other to 'those who have devoted themselves with zeal to spread his kingdom' (*MTR*, 207, 1). This distinction also figures in the second Meditation. 'God has had the goodness to remedy so great a misfortune by the establishment of the Christian Schools ... Thank God, who has had the goodness to employ you to procure such an advantage for children ...' (*MTR*, 194, 1).

With gratitude and prayer, John Baptist responds in his usual manner to this ever-present goodness which extends to the teachers as well as to the students

> Look upon this, then, as a considerable reward that God gives you even in this world, to see that religion and piety are increased among the faithful, specially among the working class and the poor, by means of the establishment of the schools which have been placed by God under your guidance.
>
> Thank God every day, through Jesus Christ our Lord, that he has been pleased to establish this benefit and to give this support to the Church. Ask him fervently, too, that he will be pleased to make your Institute grow and produce good day by day, so that, as Saint Paul says, the hearts of the faithful may be strengthened in holiness and justice'.[47]

3. 'He loved them until the end but now he showed how perfect his love was' (John 13:1)

His final gift-giving: The Testament

In February 1719, De La Salle grew visibly weaker and two accidents hastened his decline in health. He injured his head in a fall occasioned by someone withdrawing in error the chair on which he was about to sit and a further blow on the forehead from a falling door re-opened the first wound. He was required to take to his bed from which he would not rise except for the Mass that he was able to celebrate on 19 March, feast of St Joseph. This was to be his last Mass.

On 3 April, he dictated his last will which he preceded with a spiritual testament.

Brother Barthélemy transcribed it as a postscript in a letter addressed to Brother Gabriel Drolin on the 13 April. 'I feel obliged to send you the first article of our dear Father's testament which concerns all the Brothers of our Society. It contains his final instruction and the last order he has given us (the inclusion of numbered lines is to facilitate the references made by the author — Editor):

1. 'First of all I recommend my soul to God
2. and next all the Brothers of the Society
3. of the Christian Schools to whom God has united me.
4. And I recommend them above all to be
5. always entirely submissive to the Church

6. and especially in these unhappy times and in order
7. to give evidence of this never to be at variance in anything
8. with our Holy Father the Pope and the Church of Rome
9. remembering always that I sent two
10. Brothers to Rome to ask of God the grace
11. that their Society should always be totally
12. submissive to the Holy See. I recommend them also to have
13. a great devotion towards Our Lord, to
14. have a great love for Holy Communion and the practice
15. of mental prayer and to have a special devotion
16. towards the Most Blessed Virgin and towards
17. Saint Joseph, patron and protector of their Society.
18. And to acquit themselves of their work with zeal
19. and with great disinterestedness and to
20. maintain an intimate union among themselves and blind
    obedience
21. to their superiors, which is the foundation
22. and the support of all perfection in a
23. Community'.

The original of this document has been lost. Other copies exist which are very old and have variants of which the most significant are the absence of the mention of 'Our Holy Father, the Pope' in lines 7 and 8 and of the pronoun '*ce*' ('that') before 'is the foundation' (line 21).

The obnoxious truncated version given by Elie Maillefer deserves to be disregarded. Maillefer, obsessed with Jansenism, suppressed completely the passage relative to the Church.[48]

The overall structure

The detail which at first sight strikes the reader is, the threefold repetition of the verb 'recommend' in the first person singular of the present indicative tense. However it is worth noting that each use of the word 'recommend' carries with it a difference in meaning resulting from the grammatical construction.[49] Furthermore in the first instance the recommendation is addressed to God, while the two others are directed to the Brothers, as indicated by the pronoun 'them' (4 and 12).

The use of the verb 'recommend' allows John Baptist De La Salle to state what he holds very much at heart, what we could call his priorities. But in accord with one of the dominant traits of his character — namely the need to be logical, he does not limit himself to naming these priorities, he is careful to justify them. Thus we read

— *'to whom God has united me'*, which explains why he recommends the Brothers to God;

— *'remembering ... entirely submissive'* (9, 10, 11) explains why he recommends the Brothers to have an entire submission to the Church (5);

— *'patron and protector of their Society'* (17) explains why he recommends the Brothers to have a devotion to St Joseph (17);

— *'which is the foundation ... in a Community'* gives the reason for his recommendations to maintain *'an intimate union'* and *'a blind obedience'* (20).

The quite rigorous development of recommendations and their justification enables us to establish within the framework of the entire text four sections, each of which is centred on its own separate theme:

— (1 to 3) The Founder and the Institute

— (4 to 11) The Church

— (12 to 17) The principal objects of the Brothers' devotions

— (18 to 23) The Lasallian synthesis of the apostolate and of community life.

The Content

In the first section above, John Baptist De La Salle indicates that he is a 'Christian' (my soul to God) and the 'Founder of the Institute' (all the Brothers of the Society). We recognise here, as from the beginning of the text, a binary construction characteristic of his style and indicative of his logical frame of mind.

For him, being Christian and a founder are not disparate entities. His vocation as founder is simply the living out of his Christian vocation. It was in the work of founding the Institute that he lived and manifested his attachment to Jesus Christ and the gift whereby he devoted his whole being and his whole life to the same Christ. The Rule of 1987 intends exactly this when it says,

> The call to religious profession is an invitation to the Brothers to deepen the rich meaning of their baptism and to express it by accepting the new

demands that are made upon them. They strive more and more to die to sin and to live for God in Jesus Christ (art. 23).

John Baptist proceeded in orderly fashion. First of all he recommends 'my soul'—two short syllables, totally disproportionate to the long theory that follows over the next two lines 'all the Brothers of the Society of the Christian Schools to whom God has united me' (2 and 3). The architecture of the sentence suggests the idea of a Father who is only one ('soul') but who is linked to the multitude of men who come after him, and are united with him. In this way all are constituted into a single body by association, which is the source and basis of the Institute.

After 'the Brothers of the Society', there is no subordinate clause such as 'which I have fashioned into a Community'. Such a form of language would be totally foreign to the Founder. Let us rather admire the deep-seated humility with which he in a spirit of faith looks upon his enterprise as one which reveals God as the master of the work to 'which He [God] has united me'.

The second section is framed by the expressions 'entirely submissive' (5) and 'totally submissive'(11), both expressions preceded by the same adverb 'always' (4 and 11) which attributes an absolute value to them. What John Baptist is asking of his Brothers for the Church, even more than love, service and fidelity, is a profound spiritual attitude which integrates these values but transcends them to attain a degree of adherence from which there is no turning back.

Is it to be a blind submission? Certainly not. Obedience alone (20) will be described in this way. It is submission that is conscious and voluntary, but above all total, as the words 'entirely' and 'totally' would indicate. So it is a submission that is without fault, at all times and in all areas, no matter the circumstances. Yet the Founder wants something more. Practical-minded as he is, and believing moreover in an Incarnate God, the purest desires, the noblest of feelings, the most generous dispositions and even the most elevated virtues satisfy him only insofar as he can see their results in actions or practices that are often very simple but are rich in meaning. This explains the addition, at this point in the text which marks an advance in the saint's thinking, when he writes 'in order to give evidence of this' (6 and 7).

At this point we encounter a fundamental concern of John Baptist. He uses the word '*marques*' (evidence) some 193 times in his writings and the expression '*donner des marques*' (translated here as 'to give evidence of') occurs. Such emphasis allows us to see clearly, if not the actual proofs of the fire of zeal burning in his heart, at least the evident external signs of them.

The marks or evidence he requires of his Brothers are to be found in a very general formula 'never to be at variance in anything with our Holy Father, the Pope, and the Church of Rome' (7 and 8). After the words 'He has united me' (3) before 'an intimate union'(20) this double negative stands out in high relief, in as much as it is reinforced by the words 'in anything' (7).[50] Meanwhile the two titles, 'Our Holy Father the Pope' and 'the Church of Rome', leave no room for ambiguity as to the saint's orthodoxy.

In the very same letter of 13 April 1719, where Brother Barthélemy passes on to Brother Gabriel Drolin the Founder's testament, the writer refers to one of the final signs or marks (*marques*) of the Founder's union with the Church.

> Our very dear Father has written several letters in favour of the constitution of our Holy Father Pope Clement XI, which have been well received.[51]

But John Baptist also recalls here another piece of evidence (*marque*) which he gave in 1702, and whose significance he reveals, just as Jesus did when explaining a parable to his Apostles. This was the sending of 'two Brothers to Rome' (10). Two were sent, in accord with the fixed Rule of the Institute, but Brother Gerard, quickly discouraged, soon returned to France, leaving Gabriel to a further twenty-six years on his own.

Without doubt, this part of the text is the most pressing. Opening, as if between the sound of two cymbals clashing, with the words 'above all' (4) and 'entirely' (5) it unites the vehemence of the proposition with the intensity of the expression and bears witness, along with similar passages, to the vigour which affects the mind and personality of the author. If we return to the Vow formulas, we will find there already this form of absolute style.

The following sections of the testament graft as complements the traditional devotions in the Institute as well as his own personal spirituality onto this major facet of the spiritual life of John Baptist.

Fashioned in the school of Bérulle, John Baptist De La Salle centred his whole life on Christ, and did not hold back from all possible efforts to ensure that the Brothers imitate Christ: 'Let all your care be to give yourself entirely to him'.[52] Why so? In order that in their turn the pupils also give themselves completely to Christ. We have already quoted earlier in this chapter

(p. 147), one of De La Salle's most precious pieces of writing, inspired by the parable of the vine (*MTR*, 195, 3). Let us add to it this further statement:

> If you love Jesus Christ well you will try in every possible way to enkindle his love in the hearts of the children you are forming to be his disciples. See to it that they often think of Jesus, their good and only Lord, that they often speak of Jesus, that they long only for Jesus, and breathe only for Jesus.[53]

We cannot deny that these two expressions can appear anachronistic to people today. Nonetheless, when we meet up with Young Lasallians or Lasallian volunteers and listen to what they have to say, we have to admit from their unaccustomed idiom that they are translating with great fidelity what they are attempting to do with their lives today: to declare their fundamental adherence to Christ, in order to transmit the life of Christ in one way or another to those to whom they are close or whom they serve; in a word, to pass on their hope.

Furthermore these texts provide us with a lesson of capital importance —the source of Lasallian zeal is to be found nowhere else than in the love of Christ, a love nourished by the Eucharist and by mental prayer. Thus we have a lesson which requires no commentary.

We are aware of the tender and filial devotion John Baptist had for 'Mary, Mother of Jesus Christ and of the Church' (Rule 1987, art. 76) and also of his custom of affirming the important events in the foundation of the Institute by means of Marian pilgrimages, for example, to Liesse, to our Lady of Virtues at Aubervilliers, and to Our Lady de la Garde at Marseilles. How his heart must be rejoicing when today the Hermitage of Parmenie, enriched by its Lasallian associations, has become Our Lady of Parmenie.

Living close to Jesus, Saint Joseph knew the same sort of educational experiences as do the Brothers. He and they were to act in the place of fathers to children they had not begotten. This similarity of vocation establishes an immediate bond between Saint Joseph and the Brothers. So we find so many schools, so many Brothers rejoicing to bear the name of Joseph. A devotion to the Guardian Angels ranks highly among our more usual devotions since the function of Guardian Angels is likewise very Lasallian.[54] From what we read, John Baptist has limited himself to what is essential.

The same principle is at work in the latter part of the text where the two aspects of a life (the professional and the communitarian) are reduced to their two basic elements, zeal and disinterestedness for the first, fraternal union and obedience for the second. This binary construction is a magnificent illustration of article 10 of the *Memoir on the Habit*.

John Baptist could have described zeal as disinterested. He preferred to treat the ideal of a school's gratuity, whenever the question arose, as 'essential to the Institute'. He was even eager to use the word 'great' before disinterestedness, the same word which he used for 'devotion to Our Lord'. From this we can detect that he gave very strong value to this adjective which today is used so banally.

The intimate union' (20) which he desires of his followers is what he calls in the *'Explanation of the method of mental prayer'* an intimate union of mind and heart.[55] . In the meditation for the Vigil of the Ascension, the saint explains, in the language of his day, how we should realise under pain of error, that the union produces in them

> the same effect as the essential union of the Father, Son and Holy Spirit. They would all have one and the same convictions [the same way of seeing and judging] the same will, [the same determination], the same affections [the same interests], the same maxims [the principles] and practices [the same ways of acting and conducting themselves].[56]

In an age when the word 'heart' (*coeur*) included in its meaning much more of the will (*volonté*) than of feelings (the modern connotation), such a union of heart is essentially geared towards action. Because this action is pastoral, it demands of each person an obedience that is blind (20) which, refusing to rely upon reason, opens its eyes to the light of faith.

The importance of this Testament

This testament is the Founder's final piece of writing. We cannot but admire its profound unity as well as its precision and concentration. Despite his own physical exhaustion (he could scarcely speak and after dictating what he had to say, he became silent for a long period) he retained full use of his intellect. Above all he showed that he now had a perfectly clear vision of his life's work. Founder of a Society of laymen dedicated to the evangelisation of youth by means of the Christian school, he looked towards its vital insertion into the Church and gave evidence in this final extraordinary statement of his own spirituality.

Passing in natural and logical fashion from the primacy of the Church to the radical consecration to Christ, and thence to the work of the Institute and to community life, the saint bequeathed to us the most complete and most compact formulation of the Lasallian synthesis, which accords with the third of the *Rules which I have imposed on myself* and which he introduced later into the 1711 edition of the Collection of Short Treatises.

> Do not distinguish between the duties of your state and what pertains to your salvation and perfection. Rest assured that you will never effect your salvation more certainly and that you will never acquire greater perfection than by fulfilling well the duties of your state, provided you do so with a view to accomplishing the will of God.[57]

There can be no argument about the basic importance of this testament. This is John Baptist de La Salle writing to us to dedicate ourselves to a new career, but rather is providing an overall plan for all those whose careers he has already set in motion.

On 5 April he received the viaticum, on the 6th the sacraments of the sick or last anointing. In the early hours of the 7th, Good Friday, he recited the prayer *Maria Mater gratiae,* the prayer he said at the end of each day. He then said, 'I adore in all things the way in which God has guided me'.[58] After this, he breathed his last. Before long the news of his death reached St Sever and Rouen, with people saying, 'The Saint is dead'.

'The government of ten cities' (Luke 19, 17)

The Meditations for the Time of Retreat for Christian teachers concentrates on the eighth day of retreat on the rewards that God prepares for teachers in this life (the morning meditation). The afternoon meditation examines the rewards God gives in eternity. The first reward, based on the parable of the talents (Luke 19, 15-19), consists of a 'more extended ministry and a greater ability to provide the conversion of souls' (*MTR*, 207, 1), 'even in this world' adds the Founder. But even far greater are the rewards in the next world we could say. Canonised in Rome, by Pope Leo XIII on 24 May 1900, John Baptist de La Salle was on 15 May 1950 proclaimed 'special Patron under God of all educators of children and youth of both sexes, whether cleric or lay'. More than the government of ten cities, it is the whole world that the Vicar of Christ has entrusted to his care.

God be praised!

APPENDIX

God's plan and the role of the Brother in its realisation

(*Meditations for the time of Retreat*, 193)

Knowledge of the truth

In the parish

God is so good, that having created us, he wills that all of us come to the knowledge of the truth. This truth is God himself and what he has desired to reveal to us through Jesus Christ, through the holy apostles, and through his Church.

This is why God wills all people to be instructed, so that their minds may be enlightened by the light of faith. We cannot be enlightened in the mysteries of our holy religion unless we have the good fortune to hear about them, and we cannot have this advantage unless someone preaches the word of God. (For how can people believe in someone, the Apostle says, about whom they have not heard anyone speak, and how can they hear him spoken about if no one proclaims him to them?).

The Brother's vocation

This is what God does by diffusing the fragrance of his teaching throughout the whole world by human ministers. Just as he commanded light to shine out of darkness, so he himself kindles a light in the hearts of those destined to announce his word to children.

In the family

One of the main duties of fathers and mothers is to bring up their children in a Christian manner and to teach them their religion. But most parents are not sufficiently enlightened in these matters. Some are taken up with their daily concerns and the care of their family; others under the constant anxiety of earning the necessities of life for themselves and their children, cannot take the time to teach their children their duties as Christians.

It is characteristic of the providence of God and of his vigilance over human conduct to substitute for fathers and mothers persons who have enough knowledge and zeal to bring children to the knowledge of God and of his mysteries.

According to the grace of Jesus Christ, that God has given to them, they are like good architects who give all possible care and attention to lay the foundation of religion and Christian piety in the hearts of these children, a great number of whom would otherwise be abandoned.

To obtain salvation

God wills not only that all come to the knowledge of the truth but also that all be saved. He cannot truly desire this without providing the means for it and therefore without giving children the teachers who will assist them in the fulfilment of his plan. This, says Saint Paul, is the field that God cultivates, the building he is raising and you are the one whom he has chosen to help in this work by announcing to these children the Gospel of his Son and the truths that are contained in it.

Ministry

Since God ... has made you his ministers ... has called you to the ministry ... That is why you must honour your ministry.

Employment

... do not falsify his word but gain glory before him by unveiling the truth to those whom you are charged to instruct. Let this be your whole effort in the instructions you give them.

... work according to the grace that has been give you to instruct by teaching and to exhort by encouraging those who are entrusted to your care guiding them with attention and vigilance ...

... keep trying to save some of these children. Since God, according to the expression of the same Apostle has made you his ministers in order to reconcile them to him, and he has entrusted to you for this purpose, the word of reconciliation for them ... exhort them, then, as if God were exhorting them through you, for you have been destined to cultivate these young plants by announcing to them the truths of the Gospel, and to procure for them the means of Salvation appropriate to their development.

Teach them these truths, not with learned words, lest the Cross of Christ, source of our sanctification, become void of meaning and all you say to them would produce no fruit in their minds or hearts. For these children are simple and for the most part poorly brought up. Those who help them to save themselves must do this in so simple a manner that every word will be clear and easy for them to understand.

Title

… looking upon yourselves as the ministers of God and the dispensers of his mysteries … in order to fulfil toward them the principal duty of fathers and mothers toward their children.

… Be faithful to this practice, then, in order to contribute as far as you are able and as God requires of you to the salvation of those whom he has entrusted to you.

Successors of the Apostles

Reflect on what St Paul says, that it is God who has established in the Church apostles, prophets and teachers, and you will be convinced that he has also established you in your work. The same saint gives you another expression of this when he says that there are diverse ministries but there are different operations, and the Holy Spirit manifests himself in each of these gifts for the common good, that is to say, for the good of the Church (*MTR*, 201, 1).

Such is the benefit [fruit] accomplished in the Church by the instructions given after the holy apostles by the great bishops and pastors of the Church who devoted themselves to instructing those who wanted to become Christians. That is why this work seemed so important to them, and why they devoted themselves to it with such care.

This is also what ought to engage you to have an altogether special esteem for the Christian instruction and education of children, since it is a means of helping them become true children of God and citizens of heaven. This is the very foundation and support of their piety and of all the other good that takes place in the Church.

Thank God for the grace he has given you in your work of sharing in the ministry of the holy apostles and the principal bishops and pastors of the Church (*MTR*, 199, 3).

You then who have succeeded the apostles in their work of catechising and instructing the poor, if you want to make your ministry as useful to the Church as it can be, you must every day teach them catechism, help them to learn the basic truths of our religion, following the example of the apostles, which is that of Jesus Christ himself who devoted himself every day to this task. Like them also, you must afterwards withdraw in order to devote yourself to reading and prayer, to instruct yourselves thoroughly in the truths and holy maxims, which you wish to teach, and to draw upon yourselves by prayer the grace of God that you need to do this work according to the Spirit and the intention of the Church which entrusts it to you (*MTR*, 200, 1).

Since you should be working in your ministry for the building of the Church on the foundation which has been laid by the holy apostles by the instruction you are giving to the children whom God has entrusted to your care and who are entering into the construction of this building, you must do your work as the apostles carried out their ministry.
    As told in the Acts of the Apostles, every day both in the temple and in homes, they never stopped teaching and proclaiming Jesus Christ (*MTR*, 200, 1).

The chief care then of the apostles after instructing the first faithful was to have them receive the sacraments, assemble for prayer together and live according to the Christian spirit. Above everything else, this is what you are obliged to do in your work, in imitation of the apostles (*MTR*, 200, 2).

What Jesus Christ says to his holy apostles he also says to you that you may understand that all the good you are able to do in your work for those entrusted to you will be true and effective only insofar as Jesus Christ gives it his blessing and as you remain united with him … (*MTR*, 195, 3).

Titles given to Lasallian teachers

1. Cooperators with God or with Jesus Christ

Since you cooperate with God in his work and the souls of the children whom you teach are the field that he cultivates through you (*MTR*, 205, 1).

You whom Jesus Christ has chosen among so many others to be his co-operators in the salvation of souls … (*MTR*, 196, 2).

2. Ambassadors of Jesus Christ

Since you are the ambassadors and ministers of Jesus Christ in the work that you do, you must act as representing Jesus Christ himself. He wants your disciples to see him in you and receive your instructions as if he were giving them to them (*MTR*, 195, 2).

This is what your zeal must inspire in your disciples, as if God himself were appealing through you, since you are ambassadors for Jesus Christ (*MTR*, 201, 2).

3. Dispensers of God's mysteries

It is for the Church (which is the Body of Jesus Christ) that you work. You have become the ministers according to the order God has given you to dispense his word (*MTR*, 201, 2).

Let this be your whole effort in the instructions you give them looking upon yourselves as the ministers of God and the dispensers of his mysteries (*MTR*, 193, 1).

Each will give his own account to God of what he has done as a minister of God, and as a dispenser of his mysteries for children (*MTR*, 205, 1).

4. Good Architects

It is characteristic of the providence of God and of his vigilance over human conduct to substitute for fathers and mothers persons who have enough knowledge and zeal to bring children to the knowledge of God and his mysteries. According to the grace of Jesus Christ, that God has given to them, they are like good architects who give all possible care and attention to lay the foundation of religion and Christian piety in the hearts of these children, a great number of whom would otherwise be abandoned (*MTR*, 193, 2).

5. Ministers

Ministers of God

It is God, by his power and very special goodness, who has called you to give the knowledge of the Gospel to those who have not yet received it. Do look upon yourselves then as ministers of God and fulfil the duties of your work with all possible zeal and as having to give an account of it to him (*Meditations*, 140, 2).

God has made you his minister in order to reconcile them to him and he has entrusted to you for this purpose the word of reconciliation for them (*MTR*, 193, 3).

As you are God's ministers in the work that you have to do, you should co-operate with him and enter into his plan to procure the salvation of the children entrusted to you (*Meditations*, 56, 1).

Each of you will give his own account to God of what he has done as a minister of

God and as a dispenser of his mysteries for children (*MTR*, 205, 1).

Ministers of Jesus Christ

This is what saint Paul says when he expresses the wish that everyone should regard those who announce the Gospel as ministers of Jesus Christ, who write the letter which he has dictated not with ink but with the Spirit of the living God, not on a tablet of stone but on tablets of flesh which are the hearts of children (*MTR*, 201, 2).

One of the things that contributes most to impress the truth of the Gospel in people's hearts and to make them appreciate it, is when those who teach the truth, as ministers of Jesus Christ and dispensers of his mysteries, willingly endure persecution and practice what Saint Paul says, We are cursed and we bless (*Meditations*, 166, 3).

Ministers of the Church

In a great number of places in the Gospel, he [Jesus] tells his apostles, I must announce the Gospel of the Kingdom of God because this is why I have been sent. Say the same thing, that this is why Jesus Christ has sent you and why the Church, whose ministers you are, employs you (*MTR*, 199, 2).

Since it is for the Church (which is the body of Jesus Christ) that you work. You have become her ministers according to the order God has given you to dispense his word (*MTR*, 201, 2).

Ministers of the Gospel

Thank God for the grace he has given you in your work, of sharing in the ministry of the holy apostles and the principal bishops and pastors of the Church. Honour your ministry by making yourselves, as St. Paul says, worthy ministers of the New Testament (*MTR*, 199, 3).

6. Teachers

God wills not only that all come to the knowledge of truth, but also that all be saved. He cannot truly advise this without providing the means for it and, therefore, without giving children the teachers who will assist them in the fulfilment of his plan. This says Saint Paul is the field that God cultivates, the building he is raising, and you are the ones he has chosen to help in this work by announcing to these children the Gospel of his Son and the truths that are contained in it (*MTR*, 193, 3).

The end of this Institute is to give a Christian education to children; it is for this purpose that the Brothers keep schools, that, having the children under their care from morning until evening, they may teach them to lead good lives by instructing them in the mysteries of our holy religion and by inspiring them with Christian maxims, and thus give them a suitable education (Rule, 1947, art 4).

Your zeal for the children who are under your guidance would be very imperfect if you exercised it only by instructing them; it will only become perfect if you practice yourselves what you are teaching them. Example makes a much greater impression on the mind and heart than words, especially for children, since they do not yet have minds sufficiently able to reflect, and they ordinarily model themselves on the example of their teachers. They are led more readily to do what they see done for them than what they hear told to them, above all when the teacher's words are not in harmony with their actions (*MTR*, 202, 3).

Have you acted (this year), as good teachers should? ... Have you reflected that you should be their models of the virtues you wish them to practise? (*Meditations*, 91, 3).

Teachers who reprove and correct those, who commit faults, draw upon themselves the praise of people, the blessing of God, and the gratitude of those who have been corrected. For you will have done them more good in that way than if you had flattered them with beautiful words, which only serve to deceive them, and maintain them in their faults and disorderly conduct (*MTR*, 204, 1).

It is for you who are teachers of those you guide to take all possible care to bring those under your guidance into that liberty of the children of God which Jesus Christ obtained for us by dying for us. To do this you need to have two qualities in your relationship with them. The first is gentleness and patience. The second is prudence in your reproofs and corrections (*MTR*, 203, 2)

As a teacher you must give an account to God on the way you have done your work *(MTR*, 205, heading).

Harmony between the name and one's personal conduct

The Principle

'To belong to a profession and not know what it is about; is to be ignorant both of the significance of the very name of that profession which a person claims to follow and of its essential duties, seems to me to go clean contrary to common sense and right reason. Yet this is the ordinary situation of the majority of the Christians. They are Christians without knowing what it is to be Christian—and very few of them make the effort to discover what must be done to live according to this profession. That is why we believe that, having decided to form Christians and furnish them with the means of leading a life worthy of that state, it was necessary first of all to make them aware if the nature of the Christian religion which they profess to follow – and of the name Christian which they are proud to bear, of the signs (marks) by which we can discern those who are Christian, of the virtues specially required in those who are engaged in so holy and exalted a profession (*CL*, 20, 'Duties of a Christian', 1, Preface).

John Baptist De La Salle applies this principle first of all to Jesus Christ in his relationship with his foster father (Joseph) and his mother (Mary).

to have the name so admirably suited to him according to the ministry he had been assigned … so that he must not seem to have this adorable name in vain (*Meditations*, 93, 3).

God Himself has seen fit to submit Himself in obedience to you in His capacity as your child (*CL*, 14, 76; *EM*, 8, 216; *Encountering God ...* Campos/Sauvage p. 261).

De La Salle applies the principle to all Christians.

Since your Son having refused them [empty honours] has taught me to look for another kind more befitting of the dignity [quality] of a child of God, which he has come to obtain for me (*CL*, 14, 87; *Encountering God ...*, p. 287).

The capacity we possess as children of God, members of Jesus Christ and living Temples of the Holy Spirit should lead us to offer our souls to God every day that they might be filled with the fullness of the Holy Spirit. We should offer these to Him as well as our bodies (*CL*, 20, 412; *DA*, 401, 2, 4).

If you seek to please anyone other than God, you would not deserve, says St Paul, to bear the name servants of Jesus Christ, because you would really not be such, since a servant must do everything for the service of his master (*Meditations*, 90, 3).

The principle as applied especially to Brothers

Let us be sure that those who do not strive to become great friends of God by fidelity to his grace and by perseveringly seeking only his glory and the salvation of their souls, do not deserve to bear the name of Christians, much less that of religious and of persons consecrated to God (*Meditations*, 184, 3).

Is it only in vain that you have the name of Christian and minister of Jesus Christ in the work you do? Do you believe in a manner that befits these glorious names? (*Meditations*, 93, 3).

This is the good effect that your position as their teachers should produce in those under your guidance (*Meditations*, 128, 1).

You will never have for them the role of saviour, as is proper for you in your work (*Meditations*, 86, 3).

The principle as applied to students

I am so zealous for the glory of my God that I cannot see you renounce the covenant you made with him in baptism, nor the dignity of children of God which you received in the sacrament (*MTR*, 202, 1).

You will be the cause that those whom you instruct will be Christians not in name only, but they will also have the spirit and conduct of Christians which will cause others to admire them for their piety (*Meditations*, 134, 3).

Witnesses of the faith

Zeal in our work

When we are called to an apostolic work, if we do not know how to join zeal to action, all we do for our neighbour will have little effect (*Meditations*, 114, 2).

You are in a work that requires much zeal, but this zeal would be of little use if it did not have its proper effect. This, however, it cannot have unless it is a product of the love of God living in you (*Meditations*, 171, 2).

Your work does not consist in making your disciples to be Christians, but in helping them to be true Christians. This is all the more useful, because it would avail them little to have received baptism, if they did not live according to the spirit of Christianity. To give this spirit to others you have to possess it well yourself. Recognize what this requires of you. It is without doubt to put into practice the holy Gospel (*Meditations*, 171, 3).

For the future then, devote yourself with zeal and affection to your work, since it will be one of the most helpful ways to assure your salvation (*MTR*, 207, 1).

Zeal in instructing (catechism lessons)

Not one of your students should go without being instructed in his religion; it is above all for this purpose that the Church entrusts them to you. That is why you must look upon yourselves as persons to whom the deposit of faith has been confided (*Meditations*, 61, 2).

It will not, then be enough for you to have instructed your disciples about the mysteries and truths of our holy religion, if you have not helped them learn the chief Christian virtues, and if you have not taken an altogether special care to help them put these virtues into practice. For no matter how much faith they may have, nor how lively it may be, if they do not commit themselves to practise good works, their faith will be no use to them (*MTR*, 200, 3).

If you want the instructions you give those whom you have to instruct to be effective in drawing them to the practice of good, you must practice these truths yourselves, and you must be full of zeal, so that your students may be able to receive a share of grace which is in you for doing good, and that your zeal draw upon you the Spirit of God to animate your students in the same way (*MTR*, 194, 3).

At times you may have to teach children who do not know God, because they have been brought up by parents who do not know him themselves. Strive to know God so well through reading and prayer that you may be able to make him known to others, and make him loved by all those to whom you have made him known (*Meditations*, 41, 3).

The movement of the Spirit

It was rather by the movement of the Holy Spirit that these men of God spoke. It is also by the movement of the spirit of God that all those who proclaim his kingdom continue to speak (*Meditations*, 3, 2).

The truths which the Holy Spirit teaches to those who received them are the maxims found in the holy Gospel. He helps them to understand these maxims and to take them to heart and he leads them to live and act in accordance with them. For the Spirit of God alone can give us a correct understanding of these maxims of the Gospel, and can inspire us to put them into practice, because they are above the level of the human spirit (*Meditations*, 44, 2).

You carry out a work that requires you to touch hearts, but this you cannot do except by the Spirit of God. Pray to him to give you today the same grace he gave the holy apostles, and ask him that after filling you with his Holy Spirit to sanctify yourselves, he also communicates himself to you, in order to procure the salvation of others (*Meditations*, 43, 3).

Witnesses of the Christian life

Faith in our lives

Those are true Christians who live according to the law [of charity] and the maxims of Jesus Christ (*CL*, 20, 'Duties of a Christian', 1, p. 99).

Is it only in vain that you have the name of Christian and minister of Jesus Christ in the work you do? Do you live in a manner that befits these glorious names? By your good conduct make yourself worthy of this distinguished role. Act in such a way that your life may begin today to be holy and edifying and continue to be such in the future (*Meditations*, 93, 3).

It would be of little use to be enlightened by the light of faith if we did not live according to the spirit of Christianity, and if we did not observe the maxims of the holy Gospel. The main purpose of faith is to lead us to the practice of what we believe. This made Saint James say that faith is dead which is not accompanied by good works. Be convinced that the main conversion is that of the heart and without it the conversion of the mind is quite sterile (*Meditations*, 175, 2).

It is in vain that you believe what Jesus Christ proposed to you in the holy Gospel if your actions do not give proof of your belief; how do you show that you possess the spirit of Christianity? Be assured that to possess it your actions must not give the lie to the faith you profess, but rather be a lively expression of what is written in the Gospel (*Meditations*, 84, 3).

Faith in what we do (our employment)

It is by faith alone, according to Saint Paul, that we make our way toward Jesus Christ (*Meditations*, 96, 1).

Be convinced that you will contribute to the good of the Church in your ministry only insofar as you have the fullness of faith and are guided by the spirit of faith, which is the spirit of your state and by which you should be animated (*Meditations*, 139, 2).

You need the fullness of the Spirit of God in your state, for you should live and be guided only according to the spirit and light of faith; it is only the Spirit of God who can give you this disposition (*Meditations*, 43, 2).

Do you have a faith as lively as that of this saint? You are bound to excel in the spirit of faith for you have to teach children the maxims of the holy Gospel and the mysteries of our religion. Often say to God with the holy apostles: Lord increase our faith (*Meditations*, 117, 3).

Holiness

Everything about you, within and without, should reveal the holiness to which your profession obliges you … Such are the fruits which you should bring forth in the state where God has placed you (*Meditations*, 60, 2).

Do you strive in your state to achieve such a level of holiness that you can make holy those for whose guidance you are responsible (*Meditations*, 131, 1).

Prayer
as described in the *Meditations*
for the *Time of Retreat*

You must, then, devote yourself very much to prayer, in order to succeed in your ministry. You must constantly represent the needs of your disciples to Jesus Christ, explaining to him the difficulties you have experienced in guiding them. Jesus Christ, seeing that you regard him as the one who can do everything in your work and yourself as an instrument that ought to be moved only by him, will not fail to grant you what you ask of him (*MTR*, 196, 1).

These angels were going up to God to make known to him the needs of those for whom he had made them responsible and to receive his orders for them. They were coming down to teach those whom they were guiding the will of God concerning their salvation. You must do the same thing for the children entrusted to your care, It is your duty to go up to God every day by prayer to learn from him all that you must teach your children, and then come down to them by accommodating yourself to their level in order to instruct them about what God has communicated to you for them in your prayer as well as in the Holy Scriptures which contain the truths of religion and the maxims of the Holy Gospel (*MTR*, 198, 7).

In order for you to fulfil this duty with as much perfection and exactness as God requires of you, frequently give yourselves to the Spirit of Our Lord to act in your work only under his influence so that your own spirit may have no part in it. This Holy Spirit, then, will come upon them generously, so that they will be able to possess fully the Christian spirit (*MTR*, 195, 2).

This is why you must ask him earnestly that all your instruction be given life by his Spirit and draw all their power from him. Just as he is the one who enlightens everyone coming into the world, he also is the one who enlightens the minds of your students and leads them to love and to practice the good that you teach them (*MTR*, 195, 3).

You then, who have succeeded the apostles in their work of catechising and instructing the poor, if you want to make your ministry as useful to the Church as it can be, you must every day, teach them catechism … Like them, also, you must afterwards withdraw in order to devote yourselves to reading and prayer, to instruct yourselves thoroughly in the truths and the holy maxims which you wish to teach, and to draw upon yourselves by prayer the grace of God that you need to do the work according to the Spirit and the intention of the Church, which entrusts it to you (*MTR*, 200, 1).

You have exercises which are arranged for your own sanctification, but if you have an ardent zeal for the salvation of those whom you are called to instruct, you will not fail to perform them and to relate them to this intention. In doing this you will draw on your students the graces needed to contribute to their salvation, and you can be assured that if you act this way for their salvation, God himself will take responsibility for yours. Take on this spirit for the future (*MTR*, 205, 2).

A synthesis of what De La Salle achieved

John Baptist de La Salle becomes aware of a reality

1. The salvation that God wills for all is intrinsically linked to the human condition they experience.
2. Certain social, economic and cultural factors which place people in a less than human situation make salvation very difficult.
3. The lack of schooling was a factor that affected the young in particular.
4. De La Salle wanted to remedy this situation but encountered a situation which in principle and in fact hindered his efforts. The situation:

Principle	Facts	
The school was not a means of salvation but one of instruction and education.	1. The school did not respond to the social needs of the young, namely to have a place in society by exercising a profession and making a living from it.	2. The teachers were scarcely competent and especially were not motivated.

De La Salle in establishing the Institute of the Brothers of the Christian Schools reformed the school by giving it:

Its pastoral character

The school, at the same time that it proclaimed the Christian message, ensured that the message would be welcomed by suppressing obstacles to its reception.
— The school is animated by a recognized community of faith.
— The profession of schoolteacher thereby becomes a ministry.
— The place where the Gospel is proclaimed, lived and celebrated, the school is a cell of the Church, a sign of salvation, a seed of the Kingdom of God.
— The school is open to all and has a special concern for the poor.

Its pedagogy

The school seeks to respond to the real needs of youth by a pedagogy which is
— Personal: pupils are accepted for their own sake.
— Practical: pupils are initiated into living in a society and prepared for their profession.
— Responsible: pupils take a part in their own education.
— Progressive: pupils are directed in accord with their nature and their abilities.
— Efficacious: pupils progress from one success to the next.
— Universal: pupils at one and the same time develop their intellectual, social, moral and Christian life.

Its spirituality

Teachers:
— Are interested in the whole life of the pupils.
— Maintains with each student a relationship that reveals God's love.
— Teach by word and example.
— Know that they participate in the Church's mission.
— Look to God in their ministry and thank him for it.

Notes

(Please note: *CL*: *Cahiers lasalliens*; *MTR*: *Meditations for the Time of Retreat*.)

Author's Foreword
[1] *Letters*, 19, 15.
[2] *The Conduct of Schools*, p. 161.
[3] *MTR*, 194,1.
[4] *MTR*, 194, 3.
[5] Blain, vol.1, bk 1, p. 61.

Chapter 1
[1] Maillefer, p. 21.
[2] Blain, vol.1, bk 1, p. 4.
[3] Maillefer, p. 22.
[4] *Origines*, p. 25.
[5] Maillefer, p. 21.
[6] Blain, vol.1, bk 1, p. 10.
[7] Maillefer, p. 22.
[8] Blain, vol.1, bk 1, p. 13.
[9] ibid.
[10] op. cit., p. 20.
[11] Blain, vol.1, bk 1, p. 18.
[12] ibid.
[13] ibid.
[14] *Meditations*, 37, 3.
[15] Blain, vol.1, bk 1, pp. 19.
[16] ibid., p. 29.
[17] Bédel, *Origines*, p. 26.
[18] ibid., p. 80.
[19] Yves Poutet, *CL*, 48, 22.
[20] Blain, vol.1, bk 1, p. 79.
[21] ibid., p. 76.
[22] Maillefer, p. 38.
[23] Bernard, p. 296.
[24] ibid.
[25] Blain, vol. 1, bk 1, p. 81.
[26] Bernard, p. 277.
[27] Blain, vol.1, bk 1, p. 78.
[28] ibid., p. 88.
[29] ibid., p. 80.
[30] Bernard, p. 306   .
[31] ibid.
[32] Blain, vol.1, bk 1, p. 94.
[33] Bernard, pp. 306-307.
[34] Blain, vol.1, bk 1, p. 94.
[35] ibid., p. 80.

[36] Bernard, p. 309.
[37] Blain, vol.1, bk 1, p. 114.
[38] Blain, vol. 1, bk 2, p. 186.
[39] Taken from '*Discours sur L'Institution des Ecoles Chrétiennes et Gratuites*' ('Discourse on the Establishment of the Christian and Gratuitous Schools'), *CL*, 7, p. 32. This discourse is the first part of Blain's monumental work. It has not yet appeared in English.

Chapter 2
[1] Maillefer, p. 20.
[2] Blain, vol.1, bk 1, p. 90.
[3] *CL*, 25, pp. 95-135; 84-87.
[4] Georges Rigault, *Histoire générale de l'Institut des Frères des Ecoles chrétiennes*, vol. 1, pp. 523-524.
[5] *CL*, 25, p. 95.
[6] ibid., p. 102.
[7] ibid., p. 96.
[8] ibid., p. 98.
[9] ibid., p. 95.
[10] Blain, vol.1, bk 2, p. 162.
[11] *MTR*, 194, 1.
[12] *CL*, 11, p. 353.
[13] Battersby, *Letters and Documents, Memoir on the Habit*, p. 243.
[14] *Letters*, 1, p. 15.
[15] *CL*, 25, p. 95.

Chapter 3
[1] Blain, bk 1, vol. 1, p. 104.
[2] Maillefer, p. 50.
[3] ibid.
[4] ibid.
[5] ibid., p. 51.
[6] Bernard, p. 311.
[7] ibid., p. 315.
[8] ibid.
[9] ibid. Maillefer and Blain all give this text.
[10] Bernard, p. 316.
[11] ibid.

[12] See also *CL* 56, pp. 61-65.
[13] Bernard. p. 316.
[14] ibid.
[15] Blain, vol,1, bk 1, p. 155.
[16] *Meditations,* 166, 2.
[17] *Meditations,* 86, 3.

Chapter 4
[1] Blain, vol.1, bk 2, p. 201.
[2] Maillefer, p. 60.
[3] Bernard, p. 320.
[4] Bernard, p. 321.
[5] Maillefer, p. 66.
[6] *Mémoire sur l'Habit,* cited from Fitzpatrick, p. 190.
[7] Blain, vol.1, bk 2, p. 173.
[8] ibid., p. 175.
[9] ibid.
[10] Maillefer, p. 63.
[11] Blain, vol. 1, bk 2, p. 180.
[12] Maillefer, p. 63.
[13] Blain, vol. 1, bk 2, p. 181.
[14] Bernard, p. 335.
[15] Blain, vol. 1, bk 2, p. 237.
[16] Maillefer, p. 65.
[17] This text can be dated from the start of 1690. It has been published in full in *CL,* 11, pp. 349-354. To facilitate its study the paragraphs have been numbered. Citation in English is from Fitzpatrick or from Battersby.
[18] *CL,* 11.
[19] Fitzpatrick, p. 190.
[20] ibid., p. 193.
[21] ibid., p. 190.
[22] *Common Rule,* ch. 4, art. 4 (1947 edition).
[23] Fitzpatrick, p. 190.
[24] ibid., p. 194.
[25] ibid., p. 191.
[26] Blain, vol. 1, bk 2, p. 162.
[27] *CL,* 11, p. 10.
[28] *St Jean-Baptiste de La Salle,* p. 48.
[29] ibid., p. 59.
[30] Fitzpatrick, p. 190.
[31] ibid.
[32] Blain, vol.1, bk 2, p. 176.
[33] Maillefer, p. 48.

[34] *Letters,* 10, 10.
[35] *Meditations for Sundays,* 7, 2.
[36] ibid., 12, 1.
[37] ibid., 83, 1.
[38] ibid., 57, 3.
[39] ibid., 86, 1.
[40] ibid., 69, 2.
[41] ibid., 104, 1.
[42] Fitzpatrick, p. 193.
[43] ibid., 36 .
[44] ibid., 40.
[45] *Meditations,* 143, 1.
[46] *Meditations,* 6, 2.
[47] *Meditations,* 41, 2.
[48] *Meditations,* 156, 1.
[49] ibid., 126, 3.
[50] ibid., 97, 3.
[51] ibid., 135, 1.
[52] Fitzpatrick, p. 191.
[53] op. cit. *CL,* 45, p. 194.
[54] Fitzpatrick, p. 193.
[55] *Origines,* p. 62.
[56] Blain, vol. 1, bk 2, pp. 200-210.
[57] *Meditations,* 70, 2.
[58] Fitzpatrick, p. 192.

Chapter 5
[1] Maillefer, p. 57.
[2] ibid., p. 41.
[3] Blain, vol. 1, bk 2, p. 229.
[4] The diocesan official in charge.
[5] *CL,* 40, p. 94.
[6] Maillefer, p. 78.
[7] Blain, vol. 1, bk 2, p. 282.
[8] ibid., p. 283.
[9] ibid., p. 275.
[10] ibid., p. 279.
[11] Maillefer, pp. 78-79.
[12] Blain, vol. 1, bk 2, p. 289.
[13] ibid.
[14] ibid., p. 291.
[15] Blain, vol. 1, bk 2, p. 289-290.
[16] Battersby, p. 245.
[17] *Collection,* p. 25, article 6.
[18] *CL,* 21, p. 56.
[19] *The Common Rules,* ch. 1, article 1.
[20] Bernard, p. 315.

21 Rule, 1987.
22 *CL*, 2, p. 44.
23 *Collection*, p. 2, 3.
24 *Meditations*, 153, 3.
25 Blain, vol. 1, bk 2, p. 296.
26 ibid., vol. 1, bk 2, p. 296.
27 ibid.
28 ibid., p. 304.
29 Maillefer, p. 88.
30 Blain, vol. 1, bk 2, p. 323.
31 Bernard, p. 307.
32 Maillefer, p. 59.
33 Blain, vol. 1, bk 2, p. 333.
34 *CL* 2, p. 42.
35 Blain, vol. 1, bk 2, p. 333.
36 The grammatical analysis in the original French cannot be easily understood without a close comparison between the official French and the way in which this was expressed in English (Editor).
37 Maillefer, p. 90.
38 Blain, vol. 1, bk 2, p. 338.
39 ibid., p. 339.
40 ibid., pp. 339-340.
41 *CL*, 2, p. 42.
42 ibid., p. 52.
43 ibid., p. 75.
44 *CL*, 25, p. 16.

Chapter 6
1 Battersby, p. 241.
2 Maillefer, p. 104.
3 Blain, vol. 1, bk 2, p. 188.
4 ibid., p. 160.
5 *CL*, 40-1, p. 113.
6 Blain, Vol.1, bk.2, p. 191.
7 *CL* 26, p. 287.
8 ibid., p. 193.
9 The official responsible for schools in the archdiocese of Paris.
10 Blain, vol. 1, bk 2, p. 205.
11 Blain, bk 3, p. 491.
12 ibid.
13 *CL* 20, 195.
14 op. cit., ch.1, article 1; *CL*, 25, 16.
15 ibid., ch. 7, article 1; *CL*, 25, 34.

16 *The Conduct of Schools*, p. 52.
17 *Meditations*, 206, 1.
18 Rule of 1987, article 20.
19 *Meditations*, 153, 3.
20 *CL*, 11, p. 256.
21 *The Conduct of Schools*, p. 187.
22 *CL*, 19, p. 154.
23 ibid., p. 157.
24 *Letters*, 9, 15.
25 *CL*, 20, p. 139.
26 *Meditations*, 189, 1.
27 *Common Rule*, ch. 1, article 6.
28 *MTR*, 193, 2.
29 ibid., 194, 1.
30 ibid., 203, 2.
31 *Meditations*, 37, 2.
32 ibid., 37, 3.
33 *MTR*, 193, 2.
34 ibid.
35 ibid.
36 *Common Rule*, ch. 1, article 5.
37 ibid.
38 *MTR*, 194, 1.
39 ibid.
40 *MTR*, 193, 2.
41 Rule, ch. 1, article 5.
42 *MTR*, 194, 1.
43 ibid.
44 *Meditations*, 37, 2.
45 *MTR*, 194, 1.
46 Rule, ch. 1, article 6.
47 *MTR*, 194, 1.
48 *Meditations*, 37, 2.
49 *The Conduct of Schools*, p. 160.
50 ibid., p. 161.
51 ibid.
52 *MTR*, 194, 1.
53 *Meditations*, 120, 3.
54 *Meditations*, 155, 3.

Chapter 7
1 *Letters*, 33, p. 126.
2 Maillefer, p. 120.
3 Blain, vol. 2, bk 3, p. 21.
4 Maillefer, p. 123.
5 Blain, vol. 2, bk 3, p. 517.

[6] *CL*, 8, Sup. 76.

[7] English translation by Edwin Bannon FSC, in *The Mind and Heart of St John Baptist de la Salle (1651–1719)*, p. 144.

[8] ibid.

[9] Blain, vol.2, bk.3, p. 530.

[10] ibid.

[11] ibid.

[12] *Letters*, 13, p. 59.

[13] ibid., p. 60.

[14] *Letters*, 19, p. 77.

[15] ibid.

[16] ibid.

[17] *Letters*, 20, p. 15.

[18] *Positio super scriptis*, p. 12.

[19] Luke 6:24, quoted in his 'Instructions and Prayers', *CL* 17, 52.

[20] *Meditations*, 5, 3.

[21] *Meditations*,166, 2.

[22] *Meditations*, 173, 1.

[23] Blain, vol. 2, bk 3, p. 318.

[24] ibid., p. 520.

[25] *Letters*, 8, 18, to Brother Hubert on 1 June, 1706, p. 37.

[26] *Letters*, 52, 8, p. 159.

[27] *Letters*, 44, 20, p. 146.

[28] *Letters*, 64, 4, p. 179.

[29] *Letters*, 42, 12, p. 143.

[30] *Letters*, 12, 5, p. 49.

[31] *Letters*, 62, 6, p. 176.

[32] *CL*,11, p. 350.

[33] *Letters*, 16, 3, p. 67.

[34] *MTR*, 195, 3.

[35] *MTR*, 193, 3.

[36] *Meditations*, 3, 1.

[37] *MTR*, 202, 3.

[38] *Meditations*, 158, 3.

[39] *MTR*, 207, 3.

[40] *MTR*, 208, 1.

[41] *Meditations*, 38, 3.

[42] *Meditations*, 95, 2.

[43] *Meditations*, 64, 2.

Chapter 8

[1] Blain, vol. 2, bk 3, p. 520.

[2] *Encountering God in the Mind and the Heart*, p. 48.

[3] *CL*, 11, p. 350 (Battersby, 243).

[4] *CL*, 25, 18. Cited in *Rule of the Brothers of the Christian Schools*, 1987, page 15.

[5] passim.

[6] passim.

[7] *CL*, 25, 18.

[8] *Meditations*, 37, 2.

[9] *Meditations*, 178, 1.

[10] *Meditations*, 117, 3.

[11] *Meditations*, 139, 3.

[12] *Collection*, p. 30.

[13] *Collection*, pp. 30-31.

[14] *Collection*, p. 67.

[15] *Letters*, 72, p. 191.

[16] *Collection*, p. 34.

[17] Goussin attributes this letter to Brother Robert; *LA* 34 attributes it to Brother Hubert (Editor).

[18] *Meditations*, 75, 3.

[19] *Meditations*, 104, 2.

[20] *Collection*, p. 34.

[21] Rule, 1987, article 20.

[22] ibid., article 21.

[23] Rule of 1717.

[24] *Collection*, p. 26, article 7.

[25] *Duties of a Christian* 1, pp. 174, 186.

[26] *Meditations*, 150, 2.

[27] *MTR*, 205, 2.

[28] *MTR*, 201, 2.

[29] *MTR*, 202, 2.

[30] *Meditations*, 182, 3.

[31] *MTR*, 196, 1.

[32] *Meditations*, 187, 3.

[33] *CL*, 25, 20.

[34] *CL*, 18, 2.

[35] *MTR*, 199, 1.

[36] ibid., 195, 2.

[37] ibid., 207, 3.

[38] ibid., 193, 2.

[39] *Letters*, 27, 13.

[40] *Meditations*, 11, 2.

[41] op. cit., p. 117.

[42] ibid, p. 118.

[43] *MTR*, 193, 2.

[44] *The Conduct of Schools*, p. 141-142.

[45] ibid, p. 153.

[46] *Meditations*, 101, 3.

[47] *Meditations,* 39, 2.
[48] Blain, vol. 1, bk 1, p. 94.
[49] *Meditations,* 199, 3.
[50] *MTR,* 201, 1.
[51] ibid., 198, 2.

Chapter 9
[1] *Letters,* 22, 9.
[2] *Letters,* 29, 8.
[3] *Letters,* 44, 3-4.
[4] *CL,* 25, 27.
[5] *Meditations,* 160, 3.
[6] *MTR,* 197, 2.
[7] op. cit., p. 357.
[8] Blain, vol. 2, bk 3, p. 560.
[9] ibid.
[10] Blain, vol. 2, bk 3, p. 521.
[11] *Histoire générale de l'Institut,* p. 256.
[12] Rule, ch.VII, article 6.
[13] Blain, vol. 1, p. 8.
[14] 1987 Rule, article 3.
[15] A point in canonical law which allowed a person to have the revenues from a number of church properties.
[16] Maillefer, p. 145.
[17] ibid.
[18] Rigault, op. cit., p. 250.
[19] ibid.
[20] ibid., p. 372.
[21] Maillefer, p. 149.
[22] ibid.
[23] ibid.
[24] Maillefer, p. 150.
[25] Blain, bk. 3, p. 617.
[26] ibid., p. 618.
[27] ibid., p. 619.
[28] *Letters,* 30, 2.
[29] Blain, bk .3, p. 624.
[30] *Letters,* 18, 17-18.
[31] Maillefer, p. 157-158.
[32] ibid., p. 163.
[33] ibid., p. 164.
[34] ibid.
[35] Blain, bk. 3, p. 657.
[36] Maillefer, p. 169.
[37] ibid., p. 167.
[38] Blain, bk 2, p. 290.

[39] *CL,* 8, p. 319.
[40] Maillefer, p. 169.
[41] *CL,* 8, 19.
[42] Blain, vol. 2, bk. 3, p. 660.
[43] ibid., p. 598.
[44] ibid., p. 600.
[45] *CL,* 8, p. 113.

Chapter 10
[1] Maillefer, p. 172-174.
[2] Blain, vol. 2, bk 3, pp. 672-673.
[3] Bannon, *The Mind and Heart of St John Baptist de La Salle,* p. 346.
[4] Maillefer, p. 174-175.
[5] Blain, vol. 2, bk 3, p. 682.
[6] *Letters,* 129, p. 249.
[7] ibid.
[8] Maillefer, p. 164.
[9] Blain, vol. 2, bk 3, pp. 672-673.
[10] Jacques Goussin has written a brochure entitled 'Meditations for the Time of Retreat — Syntactical Treatment'. Without in any way changing the style, it divides the material of the texts into simpler, shorter and more perceptible elements.
[11] *Memoir on the Habit,* p. 190.
[12] *MTR,* 196, 1.
[13] *MTR,* 200, 1.
[14] *MTR,* 201, 2.
[15] *MTR,* 207, 3.
[16] *MTR,* 205, 2.
[17] Blain, vol. 1, bk 1, p. 9.
[18] Maillefer, p. 22.
[19] Blain, vol. 1, bk 1, p. 22.
[20] Blain, vol. 1, bk 1, p. 20.
[21] ibid., p. 133.
[22] Bernard, p. 311.
[23] op. cit.193, 1.
[24] ibid.
[25] *MTR,* 201, 1.
[26] ibid.
[27] *MTR,* 201, 1.
[28] ibid.
[29] ibid., 201, 2.
[30] *MTR,* 193, 2.
[31] op. cit.43, 3.

[32] *MTR,* 195, 2.

[33] *MTR,* 206, 1.

[34] *MTR,* 195, 3.

[35] *Meditations,* 115, 3.

[36] *Meditations,* 64, 2.

[37] *MTR,* 208, 1.

[38] *MTR,* 194, 3.

[39] *MTR,* 195, 2.

[40] *MTR,* 196, 1.

[41] *MTR,* 204, 1.

[42] ibid., 2.

[43] *MTR,* 196, 3.

[44] *MTR,* 200, 2.

[45] *MTR,* 198, 3.

[46] *MTR,* 205, 3.

[47] *MTR,* 207, 3.

[48] Maillefer, pp. 190-191.

[49] The French text has a detailed grammatical note presented in a shortened form as: 'The first usage means "a prayer to be favourable" (Littré) and it is constructed with a noun complement — as in the expression "I recommend a certain thing to a certain person". The two other usages imply "to request that attention be given" (Littré) and are constructed with an indirect object as complement as in the phrase "I recommend [to] someone that he perform such and such an action"' (Editor).

[50] The grammatical explanation given in the original French is less evident when translated (Editor).

[51] *Letters,* 32, b.

[52] *Meditations,* 59, 1.

[53] *Meditations,* 102, 2.

[54] *Meditations,* 172; *MTR,* 197, 198, 208.

[55] *CL,* 14, 12 and *Encountering God in the Mind and the Heart,* p. 55.

[56] *Meditations,* 39, .3

[57] *CL,* 15, 95; *Collection,* p. 78, 4.

[58] It is unfortunate that the traditional translation of this expression in English as 'the will of God in my regard' fails to recognise the 17th century sense of the French word *conduite* which is better translated as 'guidance'. See *CL,* 8, p. 174; Battersby, p. 96 (Editor).